JOSEP PUIG I CADAFALCH

JOSEP PUIG I CADAFALCH

Text by Lluís Permanyer   Photographs by Lluís Casals

Ediciones Polígrafa

Text: Lluís Permanyer

Photographs: Lluís Casals (except those by Martí Gasull: pp. 6, 7, 9–15, 17, 21, 24, 29–31, 54, 56, 57, 61, 63, 69, 75, 81, 89, 93, 105, 106, 121 top, 145, 149, 155; Arxiu Mas: back jacket, pp. 20, 22, 46, 62, 70, 95, 98, 108, 121 bottom, 122-123, 136, 152–152)

Coordination: Montse Holgado

Desing: Estudi Polígrafa / B. Martínez

Translation and proofreading: Josephine Watson

Production: Rafael Aranda

Color Separation: Format Digital, Barcelona

Printing: Filabo, S. A., Sant Joan Despí

I.S.B.N.: 84-343-0976-9

Dep. legal: B. 40.809 - 2001 (Printed in Spain)

With the support of   Institut Municipal del Paisatge
                       Urbà i la Qualitat de Vida

Contents

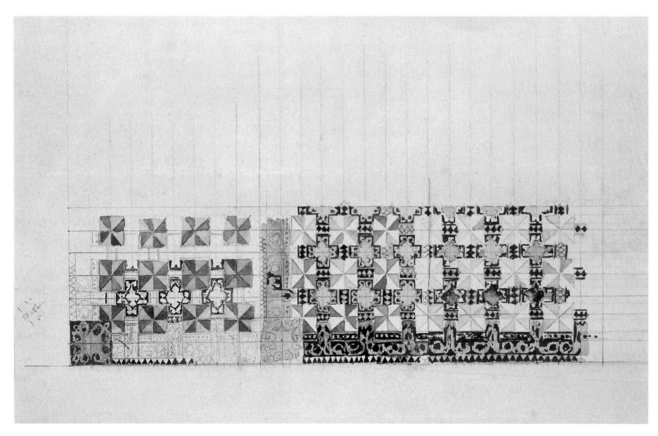

Studies for paving, undated

Josep Puig i Cadafalch: the Architect

At the onset of the 20th century in Barcelona rumour had it that Puig i Cadafalch was the most prolific writer among architects, and that more writing was devoted to his work than to that of any other architect. This was neither an overstatement nor a friendly compliment but a sententious assertion, though to be perfectly honest it fell short: in such a character everything, or almost everything, acquired an air of exaggeration, of pushing things to the limit, of overstepping the mark. In effect, his vast theoretical oeuvre and projects, his political task and the times he was re-elected to office, his unyielding attitude towards his enemies, the wide range of creative genres he practised, et cetera… for all this and much more, the legacy of such an intense life proved to be overwhelming. In itself, his own existence can be considered disproportionate for the times, for he would reach the ripe old age of eighty-nine, designing his last creation at eighty. Architect, town-planner, historian, feature writer, politician, teacher, lecturer, a personality with a fascinating talent for leadership in his private work, the flair to conduct a tailor-made orchestra and the talent of a man in public office. Let's take it step by step.

Landmarks of a Lifetime

Josep Puig i Cadafalch was born on the 17th of October of 1867 at carrer Carreró, 39, in Mataró, in the bosom of a well-to-do family that owned a textile industry.

From a very early age he showed a romantic interest in the past and a unique talent for draughtsmanship, which led him to sign up on a course of fine arts. Not content with enrolling at the Escola d'Arquitectura, given his inclination and interest in science, he decided he would simultaneously take a degree in Physics and Mathematics, disciplines in which he would go on to obtain a doctorate in Madrid.

As soon as he attained the desired degrees, he began to work as a municipal architect in Mataró; such resources proved very useful, for he was able to try his hand at different tasks while learning to regard the house as part of a larger urban totality.

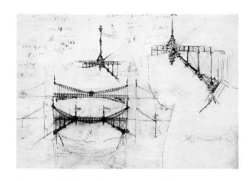

Monumental bridge. End of course project, Barcelona, 1891

Costa i Macià vault, 1902. Lloret de Mar cemetery, Girona

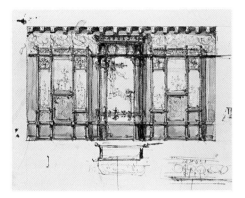

Macià Jewellers, 1893–1894, Barcelona

Anís del Mono Refreshment Kiosk, 1896, Badalona

Puig i Cadafalch joined the ranks of the Unió Catalanista and, as party delegate for Mataró, took part in the crucial historical episode of the Bases de Manresa.

The first work Puig produced as an architect in Barcelona was Macià jewellers, a shop designed in 1893 and located in the most fashionable quarter of the city at the time, carrer Ferran, while his first large architectural project was executed in 1897 in Mataró, commissioned by Joaquim Coll i Regàs. This marked the beginning of a brilliant career, stimulated by a feverish activity. During the exercise of his profession he carried out at least one hundred projects, in spite of which his trajectory does not stand out as much for the volume of work it comprises as for its unquestionable quality, as well as its innovative nature which has however been called into question. In view of the rhythm of his creative development, having reached this point we could be led to suspect that he was driven more by the idea of working indefatigably than by the urge to discover new paths and languages. Nothing further from truth, for his practice is distinguished by an evolution that tends to avoid easy answers, by a keenness to introduce new elements, to shatter preconceptions and contribute to *Noucentisme*, the cultural movement of political scope that developed at the beginning of the 20th century. Or else to design a detached house as if it were a block of flats, a refreshment kiosk (Anís del Mono), the throne for a poetry-festival queen (Jocs Florals), family vaults, the largest free-standing development of the Eixample district, a shop, a hotel (Términus) or a pharmacy (Sastre i Marquès) and a vast group of industrial premises (Codorniu Wine-Cellars). All these projects (including the small-scale designs) present the spectacular hallmark of a personality that even those most unacquainted with such work compellingly recognise. From the very beginning, as an architect he acquired the dimension of a music conductor, introducing in his repertoire the work of reputed artists and artisans, who encouraged the dazzling appearance of applied arts in his works in the laudable intention of imposing the taste for *horror vacui* shown by *Modernisme,* the specifically Catalan variant of Art Nouveau. He thus became the mentor of sculptors such as Arnau, wrought-iron workers such as Ballarín, polychrome glaziers such as Rigalt, decorative stonemasons such as Juyol, et cetera.

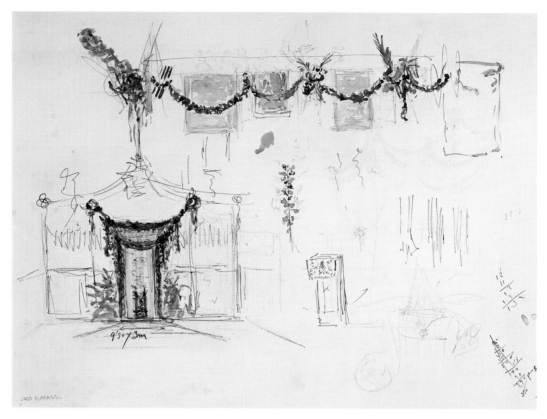

Poetry Festival Throne Room, 1908, Barcelona

Project for a Casino, 1929, Argentona

From the decade of the twenties onwards he directed his task towards Montserrat, in an operation I prefer to interpret as a rendering of material help to Catalonia's sensitive and significative spiritual centre, put into effect by its highest political representative of the time.

The Town Planner

Puig i Cadafalch's activity as a town planner was of equal consequence, not least because of the exceptional transcendence of the works. The first of these surfaced as a result of his position as councillor in the Barcelona Town Hall. In effect, he was the driving force behind the competition of the Plan of Intersections, the objective of which was to break the backbone of what he considered the intolerable orthogonal monotony that had fallen on the site of the Eixample like a weight, almost a dead one, promoted by Cerdà and imposed by Madrid. The antipathy the he felt for the civil engineer was irrepressible, to the point of confessing that while he would absolve the man he would proclaim it unavoidable to destroy his oeuvre, which he did — literally — by burning his books. In short, he was the ideologist who propitiated the irruption of Jaussely's revolutionary plan in 1901, which would not however amount to very much at all. Some years later his involvement in the creative aspect of the Reform, which led to the birth of the Via Laietana, proved decisive when he assumed the responsibility of organising the stretch comprised between the Plaça de l'Àngel and Sant Pere més Baix. His vision contributed to the evaluation of the magnitude of the archaeological findings that resulted in a new appraisal of the spectacular nature of Barcelona's Gothic past. Between 1915 and 1924 he modelled the future fate of such a transcendental space as the Plaça de Catalunya, which did not progress any further due to the absence of an alter ego in charge of the destiny of the municipality. The lack of decision-making led the works on such a substantial urban site to go on forever, until in the extreme the dictator Primo de Rivera came on the scene, which entailed the end of our artist's participation on the project. The architect Francesc de Paula Nebot would design the definitive Plaça de Catalunya, respecting the basic idea conceived

Puig i Cadafalch and Domènech i Montaner in front of the Jaussely Plan. Caricature from *Esquella de la Torratxa*

Plaça de Catalunya. 1923 project, Barcelona

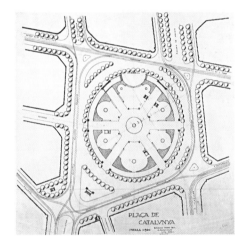

Plaça de Catalunya. 1923 project, Barcelona

Restoration of the three churches in Egara, 1920, Terrassa

by Puig i Cadafalch for such a difficult context, i.e., maintaining the recreation area in the middle of the square and circulation on the perimeter.

A similar thing occurred in the transformation of the most gentle and urban slope of the mountain of Montjuïc, historically in military hands and finally integrated in the life of the city thanks to the great adventure of the International Exposition of 1929. However it turned out that this integration had already begun to take shape as early as 1912 under the direction of Pich i Pon and Cambó, in the ambitious project linked to the exposition of the electrical industries. This explains why in such a pedestrian context Puig i Cadafalch should have already drawn the powerful artery of Maria Cristina, so powerful that its projection extended to what in time would become the Palau Nacional, its culmination. The main lines had been drawn, but he was once again relieved of his responsibilities by hostile forces, initially embodied in the figure of the General-Dictator (1923) who subsequently (1928), not content with discharging him from his duties as town planner, went on to demolish the gigantic stone columns dramatically evoking the four stripes of the Catalan flag, forbidden as was the Catalan language — a prohibition implemented by the sword.

The Writer

As a feature writer, Puig i Cadafalch interspersed his texts in *La Renaixença* and *La Veu de Catalunya*, and a number of them acquired sufficient weight to become programmatic; this was the case of those dedicated to Cerdà or to *Modernisme*, not to mention those of a political nature.

In his capacity as a writer he soon transcended local limits, for his *History of Art*, and particularly his writings devoted to Romanesque architecture, granted him a privileged position among researchers on a worldwide level that obliged him to take part in conferences and accept invitations by universities, many of which awarded him *honoris causa* distinctions. In later years he introduced a more global vision that comprised Romanesque sculpture, and according to the avant-garde thesis he put forth, Classical Greek and Roman art had been saved from inevitable

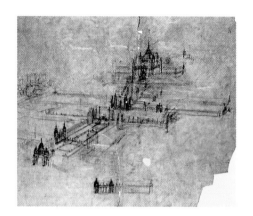

Exposition of Electrical Industries. First sketch, circa 1915, Barcelona

destruction at the hands of barbaric invasions precisely because their practice and tradition had been recovered in the confines of the native territory of the Roussillon. With the same degree of passion he devoted himself unconditionally to the immense exhumation of the treasure discovered at Empúries, that influenced him to the point of provoking an almost Copernicus-style turn in his architectural work. His archaeological instinct led him to contribute to the recovery of other fundamental patrimonial works such as the religious pieces from Ripoll, Cuixà and Terrassa, and to publicly state for the first time that the columns discovered in carrer Paradís (Centre Excursionista de Catalunya) did not belong to what was known as the temple of Hercules, as the legend persisted in proclaiming, but to that of the worldly emperor Augustus. Puig i Cadafalch enjoyed delivering lectures on such scientific issues, both in Catalunya and abroad. Not in vain did he willingly recall his fleeting experience (through no fault of his own) as a university reader, and not in vain did he embellish the information and knowledge he was still able to convey to an auditorium thanks to a uniquely innate didactic talent.

It comes as no surprise therefore, that from the very beginning and without losing sight of his roots he should have remained as attentive as possible to everything that was taking place abroad, particularly in the melting pot of Europe. I suppose this enabled him to keep in close touch with the multi-polar *modernist* flourishing and to split hairs as regards the *Sezession*. This relationship no doubt gave him the idea to create, in his capacity as a councillor of the Barcelona Town Hall, an institution as important as the Board of Museums, an instrument that proved to be decisively useful in saving the treasures of Empúries and of the Pyrenean Romanesque.

Serving His Country

As a result of his recognised capacity to conduct the peculiar orchestra of architecture and its groups of collaborators, in other words, his talent to add up, unite, co-ordinate and above all lead a more or less large group of people, he soon proved he also possessed the same ability in the public field. So, shortly after the

Exposition of Electrical Industries. Photomontage, circa 1920, Barcelona

appearance of the architect the nationalist politician made his entrance. This aspect explains that his architecture was never the exponent of a mere aesthetic; he considered aesthetics to be in the service of politics, enabling one to find political answers through the directed use of an art that, more than any other, always served the citizen and humankind. I suspect he reached this conclusion amidst his sensitive search for the historical meaning of aesthetics. Those who have assessed quintessence have rightly stated that more than a politician and much more than an ideologist, Puig i Cadafalch was a director, an organiser, an administrator. This fact drew him closer to the reality of Catalonia, a nation without a state. In other words, he obeyed the demands of a civil society at a time of transcendental missions designed to make up for historical deficiencies. Imbued with this purpose, he became a councillor, a member of parliament, a member of the provincial government and president of the Mancomunitat, a position he held immediately after having been elected on three occasions after 1917 following the death of Prat de la Riba. He did not succumb to temptations and his undeniable democratic sense obliged him to choose the path of exile before yielding to the dictatorial sword, whether it be that of Primo de Rivera or that of Franco. After the Civil War even his status as an architect was withdrawn in retaliation, an aggression that Harvard University seriously considered reporting, as it recognised him as one of its honorary doctors. For this reason it was Puig i Cadafalch instead of Sert or Gudiol who recuperated the degree he should never have been deprived of.

I wonder whether the fact of being more a public figure than a politician — as even the intelligentsia acknowledged, asking him to represent them in a tribute to Pirandello who travelled to Barcelona on occasion of the first night of *El barret de cascavells*, Sagarra's translation of his play — conditioned his lack of success in the extremely difficult task of succeeding Prat de la Riba. The truth is that his unpolished, intransigent temper, not made for dialogue and that had already appeared in connection with his enemy Cerdà, did not favour him getting along with D'Ors or with Torres García. The outcome was logical: a split. D'Ors moved once and for all to Madrid and stopped writing in Catalan; Torres García did not complete his painting of the Generalitat mural, despite having offered to do so free of charge

("No thanks, the Generalitat does not accept charity." Was the reply he received from the President of the Mancomunitat.) This was unpardonable — no politician in Catalonia at that time of national construction should have rejected the sum of personalities of such transcendence, preferring instead subtractions, eliminations, contrary to the teachings of his predecessor Prat de la Riba. In any event, he was a character who well deserved the treatment of a "homenot".[1] I cannot understand why Pla only dedicated an improvised and almost fleeting sketch to him, aptly described as a "passport photo". Cambó was generous, albeit in his own way.

Josep Puig i Cadafalch died on the 23rd of December of 1956, surrounded in great measure by the burden of silence imposed on democrats by the Franco dictatorship, the end of which was still not in sight. The architect had remained so mistrustful that he hid all his documentation behind a false partition wall; unfortunately, it was only recovered at the dawn of democracy, too late for him to witness.

The *modernist*

I will endeavour to set out a few general considerations on the characteristics of the main periods marking the evolution of Puig i Cadafalch's architecture for later, when I describe each of the most relevant works forming our itinerary in detail, it will be easier to understand his positions, attitude and objectives, as well as his need to introduce fundamental changes of course.

The design of his first buildings evinced his militancy in the highly innovative *modernist* style that was becoming established in Barcelona with irresistible force, from where it radiated to the rest of Catalonia and beyond, to areas within the Catalan sphere of influence. There is absolutely no doubt that he deliberately chose his path after Domènech i Montaner published his disturbing article in 1878 on the future of national architecture. His swift politicisation and youthful interest in looking back to the past in search of the historical keys that conditioned the

---

1. The reference is to the literary profiles of eminent characters of his day written by Josep Pla and published in series under the generic title *Homenots* (literally, well-built men).

present and could forge the future, led him to become an active member of *Modernisme* and, within this style, to choose a current extremely committed to essential tradition, that is, with the tendency that had unmistakably shaped his native land.

So, to clarify the scene it is worthwhile remembering the classification formulated by Alexandre Cirici in his time on the diverse trends. After the Ruskinian mediaevalists Martorell and Fontserè, Gaudí marked a powerful tendency followed, for instance, by Rubió, Berenguer, Font i Gumà, Masó or Pericas. Domènech marked another, which for example included Vilaseca, Gallissà, Romeu or Puig i Cadafalch. And he specifies that the latter was the maximum representative of Neo-Gothicism.

On this account his oeuvre is of a contagious clarity; we always realise where his inspiration comes from, while he ensured his influences were evident, for not in vain did he propose to use architecture, from the very beginning, with a finality that transcended the framework of pure aesthetics. If there should have been any cause for doubt, at the end of his life he categorically declared, "All my works have the same origin: a desire to renew Gothic art with the idea of reviving its spirit, filling it with the art of our days, with the freedom and independence of a new work." His historicist option is understandable, given that he was seeking the roots that matured at the moment of Catalonia's maximum splendour while he deliberately marginalised the decadent centuries. Two styles undeniably hover over the horizon of such an objective: Romanesque and Gothic. Yet their use has nothing to do with imitation, for once the point of departure is clear, he will work hard at reinterpreting it with an inimitable personality, not merely in the light of the present but above all thanks to the incorporation of the artists and artisans whose close collaboration he required. In this ornamental sphere we will see how he broadens his range of interests and approaches Mudéjar, Baroque and Plateresque art, perfecting his irrefutable eclecticism. The fact is that he considered the essence of architecture was tradition. As regards typology, it is in this context that we should interpret his constant allusions to the mediaeval Catalan palace with its central patio presiding the entrance to the ground floor, from where the solemn staircase leading to the upper floor stems.

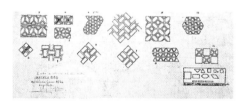

Montserrat Monastery. Section of the interior cloister, 1923

Montserrat Monastery. Study of the interior cloister, 1926

Montserrat Monastery. Study of the interior cloister, 1926

Montserrat Monastery. Interior cloister

Brick

Consequently, his choice of brick as the raw material of his construction is understandable. In his case this option is neither pointless nor superficial, and led a perceptive expert such as Cirici to name an entire period of his oeuvre. His politically-committed vision of the past, enhanced by the high level of achievement this material had provided Domènech i Montaner, did not only lead him to prefer brick but more importantly to leave it undressed, to the point that open brickwork would become one of his signs of identity. There is no need for either deception or disguise as truth, albeit prosaic, can and must be beautiful. Herein lies a part of *modernist* philosophy regarding such materials. Moreover, there is nothing like brick to provide the warmth and direct sensuality of the earth, of the native soil, while the artist's look back at history granted the quality of the works bequeathed by Aragonese Mudéjar. While sculptors used clay for modelling, architects configured their constructions departing from this unit — the brick — which offered various textures and colours, together with other formal possibilities, through its use with templates.

The utilisation of bricks in *modernist* works led Cirici to describe this period as pink. And we shall see how the change in colour announces a change in style.

During this period, ornamentation acquires exceptional relevance, obliging him to seek out a wonderful team of collaborators, artists or merely artisans. This decision was not at all trivial, for during the mediaeval period a host of hands had diligently cultivated all types of crafts, and the reputation of some of these specialities had crossed borders. While certain trades had survived, in other cases they had to be reinstated or improved, an objective that prompted Domènech i Montaner to establish an educational nucleus where his Café-Restaurant had stood in the Barcelona Universal Exposition of 1888. To name but one instance, Lluís Bru was sent to Italy to learn the technique of Roman mosaic. So, the incorporation of applied arts entailed going back to their origins but also appraising existing workrooms which, given the architect's politically-engaged views, also helped to "build the nation". It is not at all hazardous to state that the collaboration of all

Casa Terradas, «Casa de les Punxes» [House of Thorns], Barcelona, circa 1926

those artisans exerted a certain influence on shaping the young architect's style. Early in 1894 Puig i Cadafalch struck up a friendship with the great sculptor Eusebi Arnau, whose chiselling he requested on the Parera house he was building in Mataró. His desire to obtain the best possible results would lead him later on to Valencia, where experienced kilns made him the tailor-made ceramic tiles he needed to use as facing. I will not go into listing the artisans who furnished the best of their art, for as I describe each building the features of each contribution will soon become clear. At this moment his talent as a conductor begins to take shape, as he learns to promote each speciality in the name of unitary results. Frederic Marès, who had learnt to sculpt at Arnau's workshop, told me that Puig often appeared carrying a simple sketch and only one idea for the sculptor to interpret and thus solve an architectonic problem by means of an ornamental resource.

His erudition afforded him precise knowledge of the historic decorative elements he was endeavouring to evoke by means of the latest reinterpretation. He even went so far as to incorporate Gothic script, which hinders the reading of certain legends, as we shall see in the Terradas house, also known as Casa de les Punxes. Nevertheless, starting from these procedures and with his undeniable desire to update this way of introducing ornamentation, he took the same liberty as his predecessors who had sculpted capitals or the like, such as the bicycle in the Macaya house, the *modernist* motifs in the Quatre Gats or the political motifs in the Garí house. A sign which, to tell the truth, did not tally with the proverbial seriousness of the sensible architect.

When referring to the re-creative inspiration that led him to Gothic art we must specify that this is not always a pure Catalan Gothic; we note that he occasionally resorts to a clearly northern Gothic. No doubt the most obvious case is evoked by the Terradas house. These cylindrical towers, crowned by sharp calottes in the form of thorns — which led to the house being popular named "Casa de les Punxes" [House of Thorns] — are perhaps the most characteristic features of a foreign Gothic. Why would he have wanted to resort to models so far removed from those of his native land? The American scholar Judith Rohrer indicates the existence of diverse links with Belgium, yet at the same time hints at the similarity

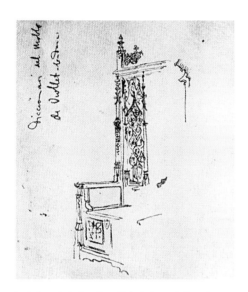

Study for a chair. Copy from Violet-le-Duc's *Dictionnaire*, undated, Barcelona

with the urban profiles that appear in the background of the Gothic panel *La Mare de Déu dels Consellers*, the masterpiece by Lluís Dalmau. In spite of all these factors that I am not underestimating, I think it is more likely that he directed his gaze and admiration towards northern cultures that, we should not forget, were the origin of our *Modernisme*. Was this not perchance the same civilised model that inspired Espriu, in the difficult period of the Franco dictatorship, to write his mythical *Assaig de càntic en el temple*? In short, historicist curiosity, aided by all he had learnt from Violet-le-Duc's *Dictionnaire* where he discovered Domènech i Montaner, led him to take good notice of Gothic patios, Baroque doors, flowered vases, Neo-Gothic lintels, and to employ all such resources with a unique talent, alongside incrustations of autochthonous art. For the fact is, to cut a long story short, that Puig i Cadafalch created nothing, either in this period or in any later period, starting from scratch — he neither attempted nor even intended to do so.

A Pioneer of *Noucentisme*

It is surprising to say the least that a significant change should suddenly appear in his work, to the extreme of leaving the northern model to one side and becoming dazzled by the south and its Mediterranean sea. This change should by no means be regarded as *modernist*, but as a mere continuation and a will to serve according to the needs of the new times, an attitude completely opposed to that of other *noucentist* artists, who encouraged a persecution complex and even a destructive mania against *Modernisme*.

Long before Eugeni d'Ors launched by way of a manifesto his *Almanach dels noucentistes* in 1911, and even before he began to launch his anti-Modernist attacks in favour of the new stylistic model from the journalistic platform of his *Glossari* in 1906, Puig i Cadafalch was working towards securing another architectural objective, one which was even more bound to our cultural and national identity. And I say working towards, as from his first attempt materialised in 1902 through the Muntadas house, until the definitive crystallisation of the Company house in 1911, we observe a number of hesitating attempts.

Josep Puig i Cadafalch house, circa 1919, Barcelona

We even notice an alternation with *Modernisme*. Were these commissions made by customers who requested, demanded even, they be designed in the style socially in vogue? Perhaps, yet we should bear in mind our character's disposition, scarcely inclined to make concessions. I suspect that double-dealing had nothing to do with either opportunism or impositions, but with trial and error, with rehearsal, given that during the early years he was the only architect working along these lines, withdrawn from all theoretical and practical companionship. At the same time, it was still hazardous, amidst the exuberance of *Modernisme*, to suggest the possibility of such a different stylistic line.

Where did the new direction or model come from? In the face of a foreign *Modernisme* stemming from the north, with Anglo-Saxon and German features imitating the French Beaux Arts, he felt tempted by the Austrian *Sezessionstil* because of its classical, more balanced background and its national traits. For this reason Puig i Cadafalch, persisting in the search for a counterpoint that would connect more directly with the Catalan disposition and respond in a higher degree to a style with greater autochthonous resonance, felt that popular Mediterranean architecture opened up new possibilities worthy of being taken into account and rehearsed. Having been erected close to the sea, this architecture was characterised by pure forms, marked volumes and large flat and often white surfaces that granted it a luminous and absolutely radiant appearance. Another striking feature of such architecture was the refinement of forms over the course of time, imposed by the typical simplicity of their functionality, devoid of all monumental excesses, ingeniously drawing it towards the human dimension. As a result of Puig i Cadafalch's attentive regard of this style we see how shortly after the aforementioned Muntadas house (1902) he began a process of progressive suppression of sculptural and even of pictorial ornaments, especially those related to the exteriors, to façades. I am not familiar with the decoration of a number of his interiors, although in other cases such as the Trinxet house (1904) the presence of *Modernisme* still persisted. So, we see him rehearse this new aesthetic proposal from different angles in the houses known as Llorach (1902), Bofill (1904), the previously mentioned Trinxet, culminating in Company (1911) and crowned by his own house, of 1907. In all these we note his cultivation of geometric forms stemming from detectable sources such as the great classics. In short, they were the houses that would soon be drawn by Jaume Llongueras, Torné Esquius and many others, each in their own fashion within so-called *Noucentisme*.

It is important to stress Puig i Cadafalch's adventure, undertaken single-handedly until the year 1913, when the outstanding architect Masó championed the cultural institution "Athenea".

We should ask ourselves the secret reasons why the attentive lookout Eugeni d'Ors, who took up the standard of the new style that was destined to sweep away for ever more the so-called foreign, northern and barbarian irrationality of *Modernisme*, had failed to warn of the appearance of these new buildings. Firstly it is worthwhile to report a curious fact: D'Ors had a deep knowledge of Puig i Cadafalch's architecture — did he also have to suffer it? Indeed, thanks to *Turment-frument*, the first book by the young poet López-Picó, we are aware that the conceited Pantarca already lived above one of those towers, for he wrote a prologue which he signed as follows: "1-1-1910 in the House of Thorns". Although the architect designed a series of works that fitted in well with the ideas outlined by D'Ors, I suspect it was very likely that he did not trust the future of such a converted *modernist*, nor a character so little prone to being guided, and even less such a conservative politician. At the end of the day the conflict between the two was really a battle between conservatism and progressiveness within the same party. The only thing we can be sure of is that D'Ors did not dedicate a single gloss to Puig as an architect, although he did give him a mention as a historian of Romanesque art. The funniest though least surprising fact, given the character's profile, is that once the split was a *fait accompli* and D'Ors was in Madrid writing in Spanish, he produced a highly original gloss to destroy that same book! He would also take advantage of the slightest opportunity to denounce what he described as a "Gothic-Puig i Cadafalchian-conscript-Catalan" style.

Leaving exaggerations to one side, it is also worthy to note that Puig i Cadafalch was put in his place, in other words, at the origin of *noucentist* architecture, by the architect Jordi Romeu in his PhD thesis on the subject,

Casa Avel·lí Trinxet, 1902–1904, Barcelona

presented in 1989 (*Josep Puig i Cadafalch: obres i projectes des del 1911*). In his book on *Noucentisme* published in the year 2000, Carlos d'Ors emphasises the issue along the same lines.

An Eye to the United States

After this period, described by Cirici as "white", he enters into his "yellow" stage, throwing into relief a certain degree of opulence and grandeur as well as an attentive gaze at the architectural avant-garde. His intentions were to steer a city which one day had aspired to being the Mediterranean capital, yet now had prestigious projects stemming from the generous dreams for the future outlined by Cambó's Lliga. In order to understand the change, the evolution from localism to cosmopolitanism and grandiloquence, it is important to bear in mind that Puig i Cadafalch had already been re-elected President of the Mancomunitat, visited the United States and even given lectures at Harvard and Cornett. So, just as he had once looked to northern Gothic and then to the Viennese *Sezessionstil*, he would now be inspired by Chicago, show an interest in Sullivan and White, and would even notice the victorious column at the West Point military academy, a model he would multiply by four — the number of trails of blood on his native flag — and erect in the very heart of the Montjuïc exposition. Once again, he would not be creating at all in the sense of starting from scratch, but interpreting afresh what is foreign, inserting elements of autochthonous art such as the Valencian Baroque, for instance.

A character and an oeuvre made of the same matter — granite.

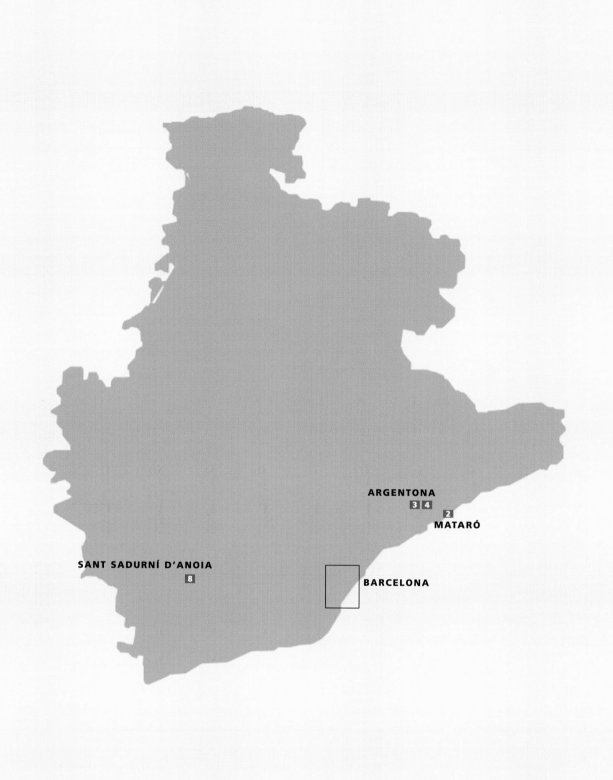

SANT SADURNÍ D'ANOIA
8

ARGENTONA
3 4   2
MATARÓ

BARCELONA

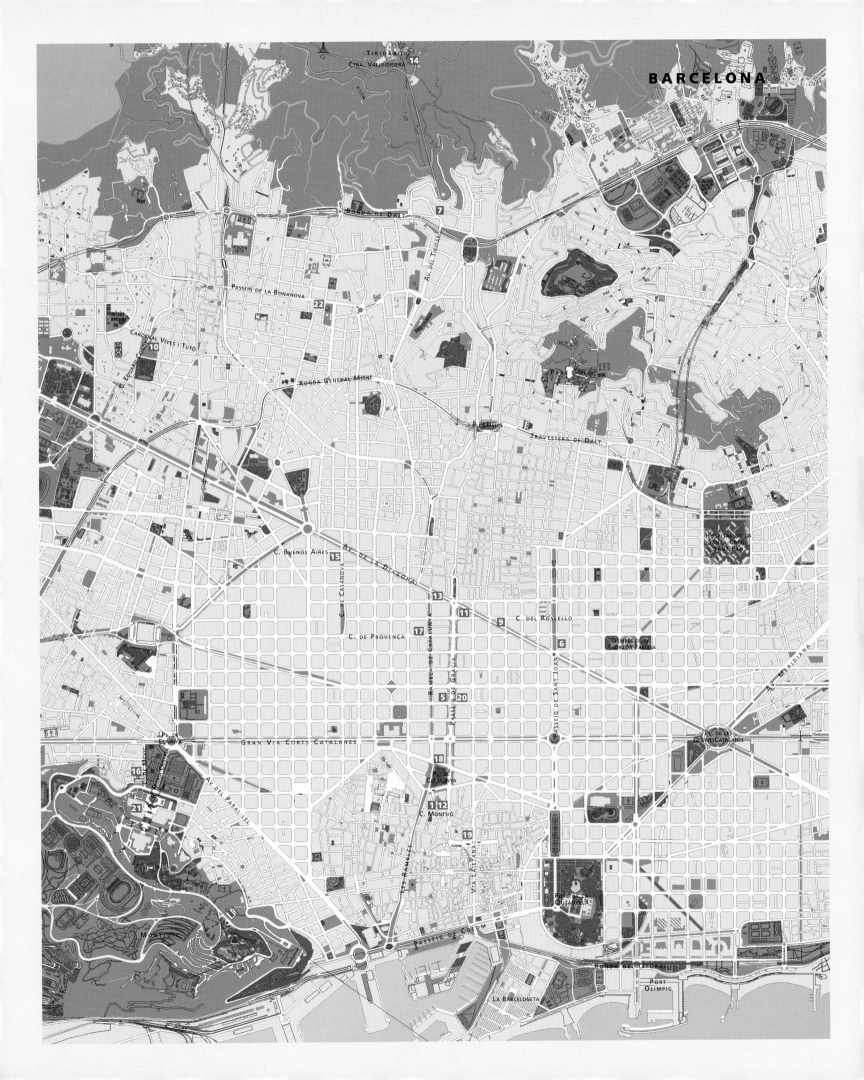

BARCELONA

TIBIDABO
Ctra. Vallvidriera **14**

RONDA DE DALT **7**

AV. DEL TIBIDABO

Passeig de la Bonanova **22**

CARDENAL VIVES I TUTO **10**

C. EDUARD CONDE

RONDA GENERAL MITRE

PARC GÜELL

PL. LESSEPS

TRAVESSERA DE DALT

HOSPITAL DE LA SANTA CREU I SANT PAU

C. BUENOS AIRES **15**

AV. DE LA DIAGONAL

C. DE CASANOVA

13

11

9 C. DEL ROSSELLO

C. DE PROVENÇA **17**

RAMBLA DE CATALUNYA

PASSEIG DE GRACIA

6 TEMPLE DE LA SAGRADA FAMILIA

AV. MERIDIANA

5 **20**

PASSEIG DE SANT JOAN

PL. DE LES GLORIES CATALANES

PL. DE ESPANYA

GRAN VIA CORTS CATALANES

18

PL. DE CATALUNYA

1 **12**

C. MONTSIO

16 MEXIC

MUSEU NACIONAL

AV. DEL PARAL·LEL

21

19

LES RAMBLES

VIA LAIETANA

PARC DE LA CIUTADELLA

MONTJUIC

PASSEIG DE COLOM

RONDA DEL LITORAL

PORT OLIMPIC

LA BARCELONETA

Casa Pere and Francesc Martí i Puig

1896

Montsió, 3 bis / Passatge del Patriarca, Barcelona

This was the first architectural work Puig i Cadafalch designed in Barcelona, shortly after having renovated the ground floor of a house in carrer Ferran, 25, on the corner with Arcs de Santa Eulàlia, in 1894, destined to become the Macià jewellery shop. Although this has not survived, the present ice-cream parlour preserves intact the spectacular coffered-ceiling, part of the wall decoration and also part of the Roman mosaic made by the artisan Mario Maragliano.

The commission made by the Martí brothers consisted of a four-storey accommodation, the mezzanine of which was intended to be the home of the proprietors. It was located on a corner between two streets, and so the space was characterised by considerable narrowness. However, the architect was able to solve this problem and to grant the project a dazzling impressiveness thanks to two basic elements — the seven elegant arches distributed at the base and the projecting bodies that appear on the first floor, that is to say the balconies and above all, the bay window. In addition the façade comprised a huge sculpture, an arresting human figure slightly larger than life representing Saint Joseph. The sculpture, which had been carved by one of the most outstanding *modernist* sculptors, Josep Llimona, would be destroyed at the outbreak of the Civil War, though thanks to the Institut del Paisatge Urbà a copy was made and placed in its original position in the year 2000. The base of the sculpture should not be neglected as it was made by Eusebi Arnau, another great sculptor of the time. Above the date indicating the completion of the house, 1896, we notice Saint George killing the dragon, a symbolic resort which as we shall see appears in almost all their other joint projects, an iconographic element that can also be interpreted as the sculptor's signature. Arnau also applied himself to working on all the artistic elements susceptible of enhancing the stone covering the entire house, which makes it worthwhile to study any particular detail, however minor it may appear to be.

The whole house was built in brick, with the exception of the ornamental elements made in stone, most of which were intended to frame the openings or merely to highlight the arris of the corner. The front door, opening on to carrer Montsió, presents a highflown flamboyant style of northern reminiscences and contains an over-elaborate coat of arms made up of emblems allusive to the textile

Sketch of the interior and of the chimney

industry the proprietors were dedicated to. The remaining ground floor area is formed by a series of seven ogival arches, two of which frame the aforementioned front door. These were the large windows that enlivened one of the most vital, influential and spirited sources of *Modernisme* in the radiant Barcelona of the turn of the century — the Quatre Gats café and beer tavern, founded and inspired by Pere Romeu, who not in vain endeavoured to imitate the Parisian Chat Noir where he had worked. Suffice to recall that Picasso made a drawing of the menu, which shows us that the place remains intact, including the interior of the establishment, reopened a few years ago. The Patriarca passage is closed — for it is a private thoroughfare — with a prominent element, the large wrought-iron gate by Manuel Ballarín, perhaps the most reputable artisan working in such a difficult speciality, who sought inspiration in some of the decorative details that single out the railings enclosing the cathedral cloister.

The mezzanine is the floor with the richest ornamentation. The balconies, covered in ceramic tiles, are embellished by the delicate railings elaborated by Ballarín with painstaking dedication. The spectacular bay window presides over a huge stretch of wall and invades, corbels and cornice included, part of the floor and of the second storey. This element will be another resort often used by Puig i Cadafalch. The fourth floor was created by means of a continuous gallery of arches protected by eaves granting the building a further touch of elegance. The roof was defined by merlons that contribute one further element to such a unique Neo-Gothic ensemble.

In this work we already perceive a tendency the architect will maintain throughout his career — the taste for asymmetry, a resource which was more characteristic of Oriental art and which at the time was only practised by those artists in possession of a greater degree of self-assurance. Gaudí detested symmetry, sentencing that as it consisted of repetition it was distinctive of fools.

Large wrought-iron gate which closes the Patriarca passage, circa 1914

Elevation of the main façade

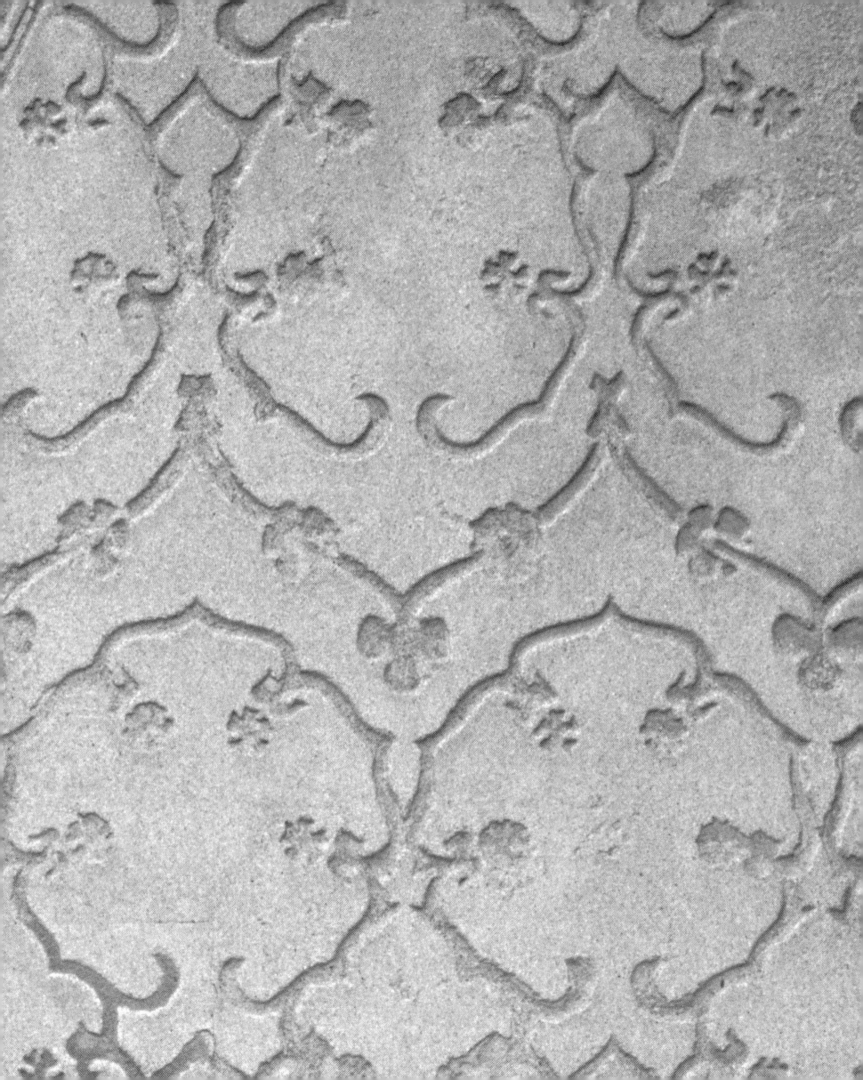

2

Casa Joaquim Coll i Regàs

1897

Argentona, 55-57, Mataró

Having been born in Mataró and being the municipal architect, Puig i Cadafalch was soon well known in the town. This prompted his receiving the first commissions of his professional career:

- *Casa Sisternes,* 1891. Carrer Sant Simó, 18.
- *El Rengle,* 1892. Renovation of the roofing in the Plaça Gran market-place.
- *Town Hall Assembly Chamber*, 1893. Renovation of the interior design. Carrer La Riera, 48.
- *Casa Parera,* 1894. This was Eusebi Arnau's first sculptural collaboration. Carrer Nou, 20.
- *La Confiança shop,* 1894. Carrer Sant Cristòfor, 10.
- *La Benificència rest-home,* 1894. Carrer Sant Josep, 9.

But in fact his first significant work was the house he designed for Joaquim Coll i Regàs, also from Mataró. The biographer Joan Bassegoda i Nonell specifies that the plans were signed by the architect Antoni M. Gallissà, even though this measure was not strictly necessary as, having given up his position as municipal architect, he was not incurring in any incompatibility. I suspect that as a result of his poor relationship with the Town Hall, followed by his resignation, he wished to break all bonds with the institution, even those that were purely administrative. Although this project merely involved the renovation of an existing house, he obtained a brilliant result that announced all the proverbial traits of his period of Neo-Gothic inspiration. By now he was skilfully combining a fair range of ornamental genres such as sculpture, glass, sgraffito and ceramics. Stone not only framed the openings but welcomed the work elaborated by Arnau, who also carved two significant figures — one in the tympanum of the door, the girl carrying a spindle, the textile emblem alluding to the proprietor's industry, and the other at the base of one of the arches, the usual and recurrent Saint George. Sgraffiti fill the rest of the façade, where the bay window with its northern reminiscences excels as a result of its impressiveness and of its layered cornice, announcing the ingenious silhouette of the Amatller house in Barcelona.

The majolica parapet, enhanced by an original design, is repeated in the entrance hall and in other rooms. The building is now the head office of the Fundació Laietana.

3

Casa Josep Puig i Cadafalch

1897

Plaça de Vendre, no number, Argentona

This work is the result of the renovation of three little prosaic houses owned by the writer Dolors Monserdà, Puig i Cadafalch's mother-in-law, in order to create a congenial austere union intended as a summer sanctuary. The architect Antoni de Moragas i Gallissà described this work supremely thanks to the delicate memories afforded by direct experience, the long-lasting impressions of his privileged condition as a neighbour. I hereby transcribe some fragments of the Catalan text he published in the programme of the exhibition the Barcelona College of Architects devoted to his work in 1966:

"Puig took pleasure in making good use of certain walls that did not join at right-angles in any corner. Although it is a detached house it is completely introverted. Being a summerly house, to isolate it even more from the southern and western sun the designer placed new façades parallel to the old ones facing southwest. He left a small separation between the two, a space where galleries are formed and which is quite cool in summer.

For many years, while Sr. Puig was still alive, these façades were completely smothered by defiant ivy and wild vine, which in autumn covered them in vivid purple or mauve shades. Fortunately a wisteria is still alive, the *Glicena sinensis*, as our architect would have said, uncontrollably winding up the wooden pergola, painting the whole eastern and southern part of the house lilac and perfuming its surroundings.

The interior of the house contains all the refinement of certain Moorish houses: a number of nooks and crannies, different levels, elongated perspectives and slender narrow points of view that are only glimpsed from certain spots, beside infinite transparencies filtered through railings, curtains, garlands or climbing plants."

If this were not sufficient, such a delicate Mediterranean atmosphere would always appear enriched by references to a number of his projects, for the sculptor Arnau generously offered him the plaster models of the sculptural works he created for his constructions.

4

Casa Josep Garí

1898

Camí de Sant Miquel del Cros, Argentona

Also in Argentona, in addition to the renovation of the Sagrament Chapel in Plaça de l'Església (1897) and to the Cros Water-Tower in Veïnat del Cros, no number (1900), he designed this house for the financier Garí, popularly known by the place name "El Cros". The project consisted of renovating an ancestral home maintaining the fortified appearance it had no doubt originally presented, even though the sentry boxes afforded it a somewhat discordant air in relation to the whole. The idea of granting the work an undeniably stately air is obvious. If he had not chosen to use open brickwork — previously concealed by the bright stucco — enhanced by sgraffito, I expect it would have appeared more directly linked to northern Gothic reminiscences. But its terraced cornice, the bay window and the large flat surface, in spite of the ornamentation, are closer in spirit to the Amatller and Macaya houses he would soon be designing. The main entrance is emphasised by a high-flown porch that betrays a lack of slenderness caused by disproportionate columns. The stone framing the openings and the bay windows is marvellously worked. The top floor presents the typical gallery of continuous large windows, all beneath a hipped-roof covered in delicate glazed-ceramic tiles.

Here is the opinion of the writer and critic Raimon Casellas shortly after the building was completed: "When visitors catch sight of the Gothic building that, standing out above the clumps of verdure, reflects its main façade in the dim waters of the immense lake, one feels one is in the presence of some stately castle, more cheerful and splendid than its mediaeval equals and miraculously preserved over the centuries." I believe this is the effect that Puig i Cadafalch intended to transmit.

5

Casa Antoni Amatller

1900

Passeig de Gràcia, 41, Barcelona

The commission made by the industrialist Antoni Amatller, the manufacturer of a very popular brand of chocolate, was structured in two phases for technical reasons. The fact is that the first mission the architect imposed upon himself was the renovation of the structure of the existing house, prosaically designed by a master builder. This was the procedure in vogue at the time, also practiced by Gaudí and Domènech i Montaner in that very spot in fact — if the Amatller house was the first spectacular discordance to appear on such a magnificently solemn avenue frequented by the high society, it would soon be accompanied by the Batlló and Lleó i Morera houses, in both cases following a process of renovation. When this group of buildings appeared before the eyes of the inhabitants of the city their immediate reaction was to christen them with the meaningful name La Mançana de la Discòrdia[1] that soon became popular.

The second part of the constructive process was only able to take place as a result of the warning formulated by the Town Hall regarding a cornice that did not comply with the regulations of the municipal bylaws. To justify the licence conceded, the following year the architect designed a photographer's studio to measure.

Once the Amatller house was completed it was distinguished with the prize awarded in 1901 by the Town Hall.

On the ground floor and in spite of the number of openings, what strikes us most is the asymmetrical connection between the two doors on the extreme left, one of which is the entrance used by pedestrians and the other is intended for carriages. Such a difficult link is allayed by the artistic work. I am not referring as much to the ornamental profusion of capitals with the dancing bear, duster or the like, but above all to the sculptor Arnau's 'signature' — the epic fight between Saint George and the dragon, prompting the dialogue between the two openings and even evincing, by means of the relationship established between the two bodies, the difference in dimensions. The quaint continuous large windows of the ground floor have been respected and enhanced by the tempting offers of the various jewellers who have passed through the premises. An almond tree appears on one of the coats of arms as a decorative motif, evoking the origin of the industrialist's surname[2], no doubt misspelt by a careless civil servant from other lands; the spring flower of this tree helped Juyol nurture the luxuriant decoration inundating the façade. The balconies of the first and second floor were composed with sculptural pieces carved by Arnau, which included the special presence of a large-format muse. Special prominence of course is granted to the stonework surrounding the bay window, that presents the delicacy of bobbin-lace. In those days the bourgeoisie called such areas "sitting cars", for they were observatories from which to gossip on what was taking place outside. To get back to the case in hand, Cirici thought he could trace the architect's inspiration back to the façade of the Saint George chapel in the Palace of the Generalitat. This ensemble must be interpreted as a personal re-creation of Catalan Gothic ancestral homes, though the historicist surprise that Puig i Cadafalch reserved visitors was the unexpected, spectacular and daring cornice, in these atmospheres at least, for the terraced gable seems to have been literally transported from an ancestral house in the Low Countries. The wrought-iron work on the balcony railings and on the repeated pulleys is exceptional. The design of the shutters is very original and appropriate, of an unusual tender green colour.

The ground entrance is well worth a visit. The floor of this hall for carriages was covered with the same tiles the Town Hall used for pavements, although here the floor-tile model was designed to measure; it is a shame that it has suffered unjustifiable deterioration. On the right we find the well, enclosed by a beautiful polychrome stained-glass window, and the solemn staircase leading to the proprietor's residence, now housing a museum, the Institut Amatller d'Art Hispànic and the Arxiu Fotogràfic Mas. At the end of the entrance hall the information office of the *Modernisme* route has just opened.

Here is the impressive list of those who made this brilliant display of applied arts possible: Eusebi Arnau, sculpture; Alfons Juyol, ornamental sculpture; Franzi Hermanos, marble; Joan Paradís, sgraffiti; Esteve Andorrà and Manuel Ballarín, wrought-iron; Masriera i Campins, bronze; Son of J. Pujol and Torres Mauri, ceramics; Casas i Bardés, carpentry; Joan Coll, plaster; Escofet, paving; Mario Maragliano, mosaic; Gaspar Homar, furniture; Miret i Ascens and Antoni Tàpies, lights.

---

1. The expression is a play on words, *manzana* designating both an apple and a block of buildings in Spanish, yet neither of the two in Catalan (despite the spelling). In this case, the "apple of discord", the subject of dissension, applies to the disparate style of the houses on this particular block.

2. Amatller very likely being a misspelling of Ametller, a surname deriving from *ametller*, an almond tree and also a receptacle in which almonds are served.

Sketches of different tiles

Perspective of the main façade

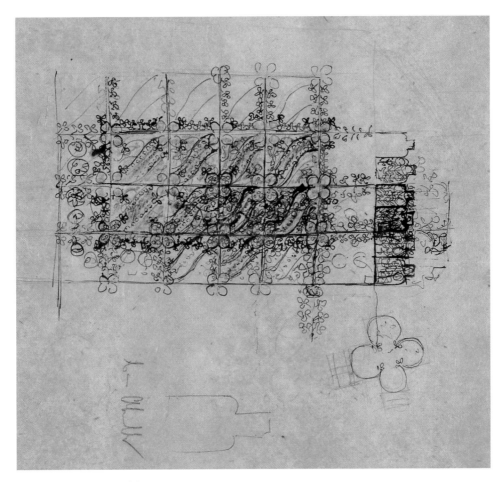

Sketch of the entrance hall skylight

6

Casa Romà Macaya

1901

Passeig de Sant Joan, 108, Barcelona

This house received a mention by the jury chosen to award the Town Hall prize to the best house designed in 1901. I suspect that the reason why it did not receive the First Prize was not so much that it was not deemed worthy — as the winner, Casa Juncadella by the architect Sagnier, was not incontrovertible — but because it wasn't too original and was also less outstanding than others, at least as regards the façade though not the patio. I mean it is unavoidable to think back and compare it to the Amatller house. Except for the cornice, the resemblance provides food for thought as the structure, the composition of the openings, the two rows of continuous windows on the first and fourth floors, and even the two asymmetrical doors on the left — a problem he solves with a greater degree of classicism — are identical. It is worth our while to draw attention to a picturesque detail that nevertheless shows how extremely busy Puig i Cadafalch was at that time. It is well known that Arnau carved the motifs following the architect's plastic indications. Well, the carriage entrance door on the left has a capital showing a prominent character wearing a straw hat and riding a bicycle, which is in fact an amusing portrait of the architect himself; he had a reputation of being an untiring worker, as a result of all the work involved in visiting the sites of the two houses simultaneously under construction, Amatller and Macaya, so in order to gain time he travelled about the streets of the Eixample on those two swiftly moving wheels. This could explain why his design was made at one fell swoop, the most creative aspect of which was the interior. It is noteworthy to justify this for while, as mentioned, in the Amatller house he limited himself to renovate an existing house, in this case he created a new building, which granted him absolute freedom. The entrance hall and the bright well enclosing the staircase offer attractive and elegant structural and decorative solutions.

It is a shame that this small town palace should have housed a school for the deaf and dumb, for this brought about a mutilation of the interior typology and ornamentation. At a later date it would become the exhibition hall of La Caixa Foundation.

The architect and critic Pujol i Brull praised Puig i Cadafalch's talent for having been able to grant "a building of domestic use, and therefore with scarcely

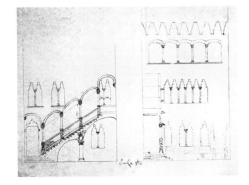

Elevations of the entrance hall

adequate exterior forms, a completely different vibrant nature, in spite of the indispensable roof railing, the equally precise rows of balconies on each floor and the other circumstances hindering the architect's freedom to act. In this struggle he has proved victorious, thanks above all to his sincerity, possessing such a gift his works will reflect his image."

Documents prove his collaborators, in the field of applied arts, were Eusebi Arnau, sculpture; Alfons Juyol, ornamental sculpture; Joan Paradís, sgraffiti; Pujol i Bausis, ceramics; Esteve Andorrà and Manuel Ballarín, forging; Marcel·lí Gelabert, decorative painting.

Perspective of the main façade

7

Casa Lluís Muntadas

1902

Avinguda Tibidabo, 48, Barcelona

A simple and at once delicate detached villa, built on the newly-opened avenue of the great housing development promoted by doctor Salvador Andreu, the man who brought about the transformation of the Tibidabo mountain peak and of this particular slope. Once again, this project is a renovation of an existing construction, although the architect possessed a recognised talent to extract an attractive outcome, despite working with restrictions. In this case the project assumes a unique transcendence, not so much for the work in itself but because, familiar as we are with his global trajectory, we are able to interpret what it announces. Indeed, Puig i Cadafalch began to rehearse what would entail the abandonment of *Modernisme* and the beginning of a style that would be christened by D'Ors as *Noucentisme*. For this reason, once again the architect turns back to the past, to local history, seeking inspiration in the delightful Baroque cornices of Catalan country houses. He is not unfamiliar with the play on curves and counter-curves in such houses, not having completely renounced the *modernist* creed, just as he had not forsaken the gentle waves in the floral ornamentation of the sgraffiti. His attempt to penetrate a new vocabulary is quite clear, as is the foreign clue provided by Olbrich, indicating the presence of the *Sezession*. From a few recently discovered drawings we gather that part of the design involved erecting a tower; although it was not realised, this architectural element would soon appear in the projects inscribed in his newly-adopted style.

Sketch of the exterior and of the ground plan

8

Codorniu Cellars and Can Codorniu Villa

1904-1915

Sant Sadurní d'Anoia

In 1898 Manuel Raventós, the owner of a wine-producing property that had been in the same family for centuries, approached the young architect with the commission to build an ambitious extension of the installations. This was a timely occasion, for an economic crisis caused by the epidemiological outbreak of phylloxera had just been overcome. Puig i Cadafalch's involvement was not made effective until 1904, when he designed a strictly industrial set of buildings, materialised in the porch for the presses, the large winery and the shipment hall.

The architect had shown quite an interest in collaborating on this project, no doubt to prove that some of his theories were also applicable to industrial needs. He thereby demonstrated the feasibility of introducing classical structural solutions, as in the case of a network of buildings that evoke those that the Gothic masters had gradually erected at the Barcelona shipyard. Puig i Cadafalch would not use stone but basically brick. Although some authors have referred to a demand possibly made by his client, both on financial grounds and because he himself had a tile factory, I think the architect chose brick for purely constructional and aesthetic reasons. The outcome was dazzling, as was to be expected in view of the austerity and simplicity; to some extent it exemplified the theory of "less is more", albeit viewed from a different angle. Before a work of this intensity, what proves most impressive is the force of space and void linked by a mere play of arches, alongside the relevance assumed by materials.

Another commission was the new ancestral home with its northern Neo-Gothic profile, erected on a square ground plan, where the circular tower that grows on the angle, crowned by its characteristic ridge, affords the ensemble an elegance that the generous projection of the eaves would not have achieved on its own. The interior was embellished by the collaboration of the Modernist Llimona brothers, Joan the sculptor and Josep the painter. Francesc Esclusa also took part in the work, preparing the sketches of the designs executed by the glazier.

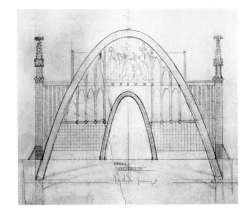

Elevation of the façade

9

Casa Bartomeu Terradas i Brutau

1905

Diagonal, 416-420 / Bruc, 141-143 / Rosselló, 260-262, Barcelona

The estate that Bartomeu Terradas i Brutau inherited upon the death of his father, Bartomeu Terradas i Mont, enabled him to devote this impressive site to accommodations in one building with a unified appearance in order for it to be divided into equal parts and passed down to his three daughters, Anna, Josepa and Rosa. This granted Puig i Cadafalch no doubt the most tempting and spectacular opportunity of building in the Eixample, for what was usually the case in that district, as in most of the city, was to have to construct between party walls as paradigmatically proven by the Liceu, the Palau de la Música and the Pedrera. A free-standing complex of this magnitude was put to the best possible advantage to design a strikingly attractive building, affectionately called by the citizens of Barcelona "Casa de les Punxes" (House of Thorns).

To a certain degree the architect referred back to the model of the Martí house, using basically two materials — brick and stone — to obtain a Neo-Gothic result with clearly northern connotations. The foreign allusion is obviously intensified by no less than six towers that form the powerful framework supporting such a huge edifice. The six large, tall and slender cylinders were crowned by calottes with finely thrown spires, which led to the epithet given it by the people. The tower facing south acts a tributary tower, being the highest and more epic of them all and containing different and larger ornamentation that enabled it to become almost a façade; this prominence has been enhanced by the little square the Town Hall has erected in front of it. As in the Martí house, the delicate stonework is responsible for emphasising the openings. The ground floor is also structured by means of a strong rhythm of arches. On this occasion, Puig i Cadafalch's proverbial weakness for bay windows presents a unique novelty, for those that appear in vertical continuity covering almost the entire length of the façade are of triangular shape. A significant part of the decoration was entrusted to pediments comprising large ceramic soffits. The distance from the ground and the Gothic lettering thwart our reading of what was written on the legends. The sun dial states, *Nunquam te crastina fallet hora* (May the hour never fail you tomorrow morning). The one showing Saint George fighting the dragon is easier to understand, as it was written in Catalan, *Sant patró de Catalunya, torneu-nos la*

Study of an alternative façade

llibertat (Patron Saint of Catalonia, Restore Our Freedom). Being intelligible and vindicatory this message did not go unheeded. The professional demagogue and politician Lerroux stood up for wounded representativeness and writing in *El Progreso* on the 10th of November of 1907 under the title "Separatismo i arquitectura", accused Puig i Cadafalch of nothing short of "crimes against the nation". Exactly!

Mention must be made of the work of Enric Monserdà, to whom the proprietor also entrusted the mission of selecting and co-ordinating the different artisans who would contribute the best of their respective trades. These were Alfons Juyol, ornamental sculpture; Manuel Ballarín, wrought-iron; Masriera i Campins, brass work of the doors; Eudald Amigó, stained-glass windows; Enric Monserdà, tiling.

10

Casa doctor Francesc Sastre i Marquès

1905

Eduard Conde, 44 / Cardenal Vives i Tutó, Barcelona

This project of a town villa for the well-known pharmacist had to be adapted to a building that, despite giving on to two streets, was of an awkward shape. The architect decided to place the garden in the sharp prow, erecting in its angle a delightful wooden arbour that must certainly have drawn the attention of passers-by. The detached house is made up of three terraced sections. On the highest one he placed the interior façade so to speak, inscribing the date 1905 on its wall surrounded by sgraffiti of floral motifs. The wooden bay window comprises two floors and is prolonged by a tower crowned by a calotte that relates to that of the arbour; while the former is covered in glazed ceramic tiles, the latter presents a fragile set of green and red tiles. In the next section, on a lower level, there is a chimney that would befit those on the roof of the Güell Palace. The third section, the lowest of all, also serves the purpose of a terrace. All this is bordered with merlons of red brick, a colour that alternates with the white stucco covering the façades, particularly the one that gives on to carrer Cardenal Vives i Tutó where a socle of unhewn stone is covered by a facing of large soffits chequered by green and white square tiles, the same as those used on the calotte of the arbour.

In the seventies a suggestion was made to knock the house down, which favoured it being included in the catalogue of works of cultural heritage. However it is a pity that the garden should be better looked after than the villa.

Almost simultaneously, Puig i Cadafalch planned the renovation of the old house situated in carrer Hospital, 109 that also belonged to doctor Sastre i Marqués. On the façade he placed garlands to ornate the openings, while on the ground floor, forming a corner with carrer Cadena, he placed the pharmacy, characterised by the typographic design of the name of the establishment and the wrought-iron lamppost that emphasised the angle, quite likely made by Ballarín. The restoration of the Raval district also condemned this building, in spite of it being catalogued. The Town Hall merely decided to keep its most characteristic elements in storage.

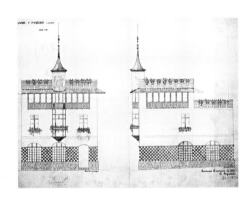

Elevations of the main and side façades

11

Palau Baró de Quadras

1906

Diagonal, 373 / Rosselló, 279, Barcelona

Manuel Quadras i Feliu, Baron Quadras, was very pleased with the restoration of the country house he possessed near Hostalrich, in Maçanés, undertaken by Puig i Cadafalch between 1900 and 1903. He had transformed it into a castle, precisely what the Baron desired after having been awarded his title by the reigning Queen. As a result he decided to entrust him with the project of renovating a house with one façade opening on to the Diagonal and another on to carrer Rosselló. The architect knew how to act, even when it came to granting an ordinary house the appearance of a palace.

Even though the building was not very appealing, for its façade only measured twelve metres, he was able to award it a striking yet not too flamboyant appearance. The whole area opening on to the Diagonal avenue was constructed in carved stone, which was not very common in a city not usually drawn to appearances or architectural illusion. The originality of the outcome was a direct result of the presence of one of the most spectacular bay windows of the *modernist* period, for which he required the skill of his regular collaborators, Arnau and Juyol. On a delicately chiselled background, the former sculpted a series of busts of mediaeval taste, a setting the *nouveau* aristocrat was no doubt expecting. The masterpiece is of course the 'signature', even though in this case it more than exceeds anything made before. Indeed, in each arris of the aforementioned bay window the sculptor represented Saint George at the instant he slayed the dragon and the malign spirits with his sword. Yet once in position, the result was an almost circus-like equilibrium, for the scene was very narrow. A dark roof with a pronounced slant and eaves, dormer windows, timber gables of Alsatian inspiration and glazed ceramic decoration provide the contrast that counterbalances such a powerful volume. The door is a remarkable piece of work by Ballarín while the entrance hall, albeit simple, is of a great ornamental sumptuousness.

The rear façade, without concealing its origin, shows delightful sgraffiti endowed with a generous floral polychrome, concentrated on the cornice and on several friezes. The continuous bay window runs sideways along three balconies, and vertically covers four floors; he bravely decided to assign a prosaic shutter the

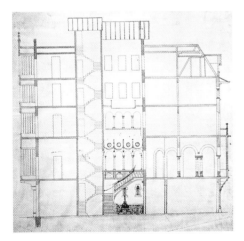

Longitudinal section

mission of forming the most conspicuous part of this façade. The door, made of wrought iron and glass, was also Ballarín's work.

A text published in the review *Ilustració Catalana*, a mere caption to a photograph of the Baroness and her daughter in the brand new mansion, helped to restore the flavour of an era: "Sweet Maria de Quadras, a living trembling flower, soft and aromatic among so many other immobile petrified flowers, helps her kind mother the Baroness in the pleasant task of removing, with appropriate smiles, all the magnificence of that home where Catalan art vibrates in all its manifestations."

For the past few decades it has housed the Museu de la Música.

12

Casa Carreres i Martí

1906

Montsió, 5 / Passatge del Patriarca, 4-A, Barcelona

The renovation of this house is only attributed to Puig i Cadafalch in the catalogue of cultural heritage, without providing any further evidence. We should note that the letter "M" that appears on the lintel is the same one we find on the neighbouring Martí house, which leads us to believe in the existence of family ties between the two households. This would explain that even though the house is usually known as Carreres, emphasis should have been given to the second surname, which could have been to the benefit of the property. Be that as it may, it was necessary to dignify this house, for not in vain did it face the Martí house and both were connected by a fine wrought-iron railing made by Ballarín. Above a socle of unhewn stone emerges a rhythm of basket arches with column divisions that set up a dialogue with the pointed arches opposite. The entire first floor is covered in polychrome mosaic, while the rest of the façade is stuccoed in ochre and enhanced by floral sgraffiti. Mention should be made of the delicate wrought-iron work of the handrails, quite likely made by Ballarín. At number 4 on the same passage a ceramic soffit depicts Saint Eloy, framed in stippled stone, while the house next door, 4 A, presents a similar soffit featuring Saint Joachim. Although the façades are different, the sgraffito they have in common provides an element of harmony. The two works have been restored in the year 2001 and now have a marvellous appearance.

An interesting city detail worthy of bearing in mind is the fact that when the ground floor of the Martí house was used as a storage space, a group of Barcelona residents gathered and founded the Quatre Gats café there. Before the impossibility of recovering the original site, they took hold of what was closer at hand, which was the ground floor of this house. Once it was able to free itself of such a prosaic fate, the Quatre Gats returned to its own terrain, though a café-bar remains open on the premises as a testimony of the characteristic public-spiritedness of those politically-engaged past decades.

13

Casa Pere Serra i Pons

1908

Rambla de Catalunya, 126, Barcelona

Even though the year 1908 does not usually appear as the date this work was finished, the truth is that this pretentious house was not only never completed but its proprietor would never even live in it. In spite of not having been finished, it was included in the annual competition organised by the Town Hall, which it obviously did not win although it did deserve a mention by the jury. The building work began in 1903 and was an ambitious project, for the façades of stippled stone gave on to three streets — Rambla de Catalunya, where the front door was, Avinguda Diagonal and carrer Còrsega. The rear had a terrace and a large garden. At the end of the Civil War this piece of land was surrendered in order to build a sizeable extension, as the house had been sold to a convent school of the order St Teresa. This work was directed by the architect Josep Maria Pericas, under the supervision of Puig i Cadafalch himself. In the mid sixties the community tried to have the house pulled down to favour the sale of the plot of land, though the idea was not accepted. After a long-drawn out and complex negotiation a decision was reached, according to which the modern annex would be disposed of to allow the erection of the adjacent contemporary building, designed by the architects Federico Correa and Alfonso Milà. The whole development became the headquarters of the Diputació de Barcelona (Regional Council). I cannot help mentioning a curious episode of a unique sentimental intensity — the Mother Superior and the municipal architect negotiating the valuation fell in love, as a result of which she decided to renounce her vows and marry him.

Driven by his admiration for the Catalan architectonic past, Puig i Cadafalch determined to pay a personal tribute to the Barcelona Renaissance period which, already presenting signs of decadence, was characterised by a virtually inexistent constructional activity. The best private building of this style was the Gralla Palace, located on the smooth corner of the streets Portaferrissa and Cucurulla, which was knocked down for shameful speculative reasons in the mid-nineteenth century, after protests by citizens had proven to no avail. Well, the front door of the Serra house is an interpretation of the door adorning the Gralla Palace, including the door-knocker which was stolen when the building was restored and extended; the present knocker is completely different. Puig asked Arnau to carve a saw on the

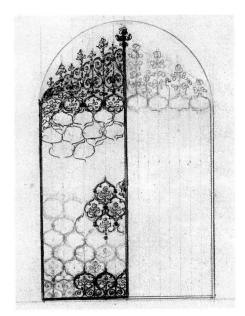

Sketch of the gate of the Diagonal façade

storiated coat of arms, in an allusion to the proprietor's surname[1]. On the other hand, all the medallions of the windows contain the sculpted heads of personages such as Wagner, Cervantes, Fortuny and others of similar rank. The powerful eaves are supported by fine wrought-iron work by Manuel Ballarín, who also created the delicate and elaborate continuous railings of the balconies. The glazed ceramic tiles grant a touch of colour to the roof, as does the spire crowning the cylindrical tower that harks back to the model used in Casa de les Punxes. Once again, Alfons Juyol was responsible for all the stone ornamentation.

Sketch of the façade

1. The Catalan for 'saw' is *serra*.

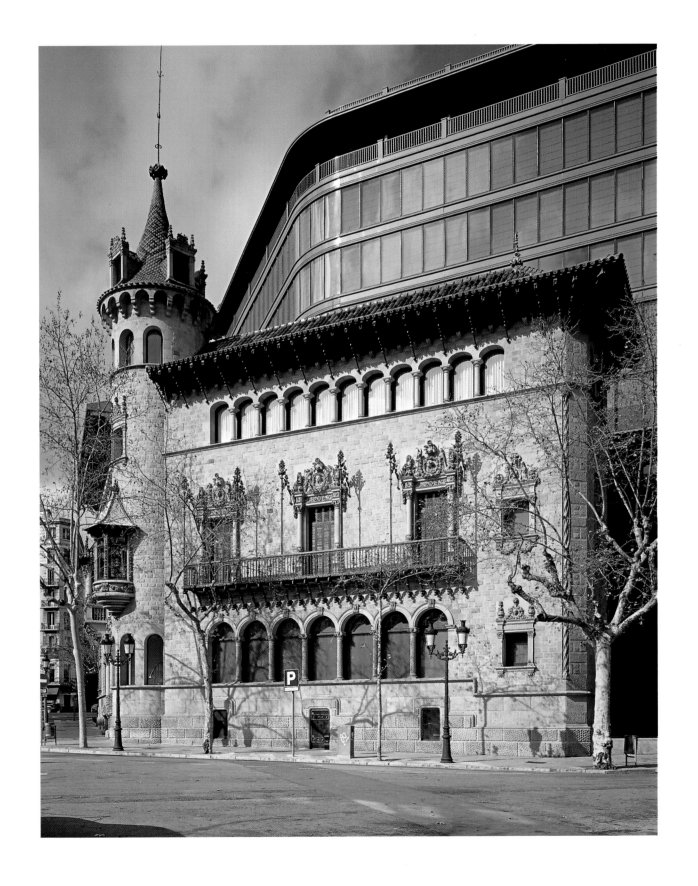

14

Casa Mercè Pastor de Cruylles

1908

Tibidabo, Barcelona

The marchioness of Castell de Torrent commissioned a sort of studio-villa to be constructed at the peak of the Tibidabo. It was a solid edifice, constructed in unhewn ashlar, which emphasised its tribute to the most austere autochthonous Gothic style. Cirici reports that it could perfectly well have been taken for an essential fifteenth-century ancestral home were it not for the fishplate of its façades, which the architect had no doubt picked up from the Visigothic remains of our country during his research of the history of its architecture. In his PhD thesis, the architect Jordi Romeu is more precise and declares that at the time Puig was writing the first volume of his work devoted to Roman architecture, which would explain the signs of this influence in his reflections on stone, arches, lintels and the distribution of materials. And he goes on to add that as a whole, the appearance of the house is reminiscent of a belvedere tower, which undoubtedly constitutes a reference to watch-towers. Not the slightest ornamental concession can be observed, not even in the frames of the large windows; his only indulgence was the well-known resort of the eaves, of unusual dimensions, granting the roof a strength and prominence that almost cancels out the presence of the solution given to the top floor, composed of a gallery of continuous large windows of extreme simplicity.

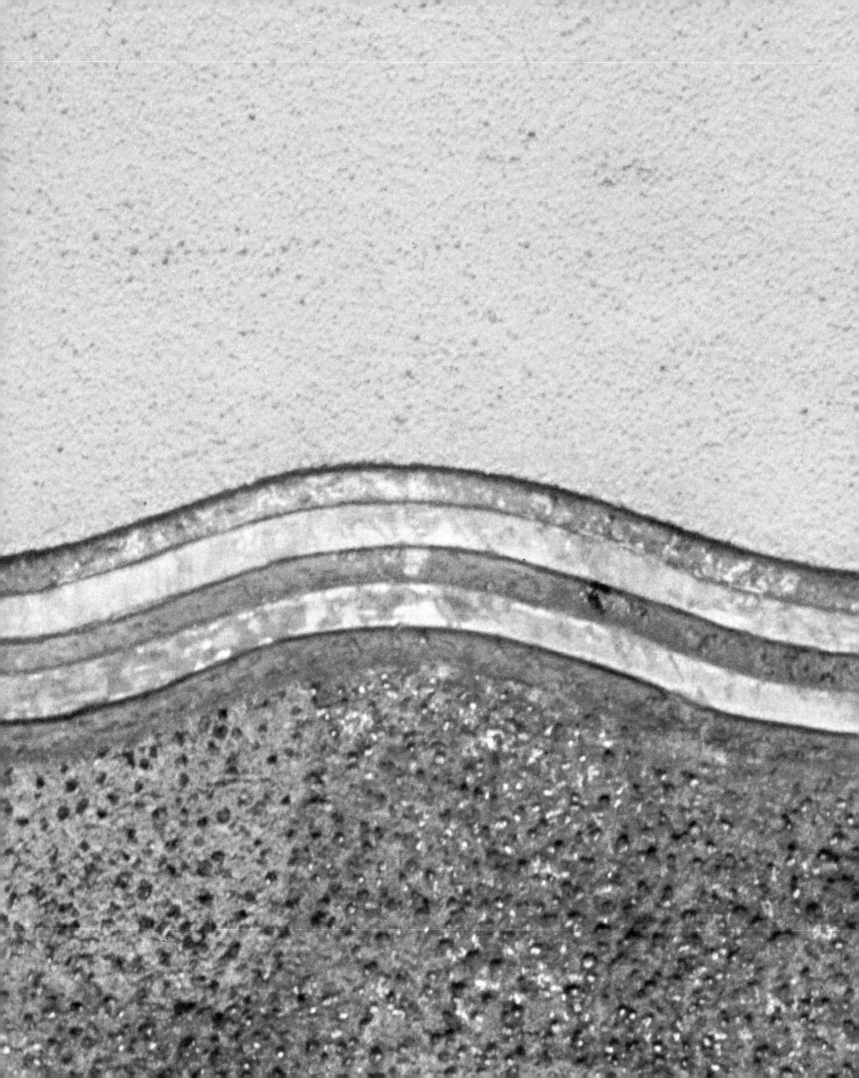

15

Casa Pere Company

1911

Casanova, 203 / Buenos Aires, Barcelona

This was an undemanding space where Puig i Cadafalch designed what would eventually be regarded as the first *noucentist* house. This work is easier to understand if we take into account certain precedents that, more than vacillations, betray attempts to find this new path that appeared to have greater links to tradition and to the spirit of these surroundings. So, it is almost mandatory to evoke the aforementioned Muntadas house (1902) and the house of Concepció Dolsa, widow of Llorach (Muntaner, 263 / Travessera, no longer standing). All these houses show the rehearsal of styles, some stemming from the Viennese *Sezession*, others from the Catalan Baroque, though not in a pure state but subtly blended and filtered through the architect's own personality. Yet the style and assurance shown in the Pere Company house would no doubt have a lasting influence. The architect Romeu believes that the *Sezessionstil* influence is indebted to Olbrich whom he does not hesitate in describing as Puig i Cadafalch's second father. Although these influences are clear, the global appearance is integrated in the Catalan atmosphere to the point that it would not be out of place in a drawing by Torné Esquius or by Obiols.

This was the last family residence designed by Puig i Cadafalch, with its detached tower and surrounding garden, the most outstanding features of which are the colour white, the straight lines and right angles and the austerity and clarity. On top of an unhewn stone socle he designed a well-defined simple volume with a number of small openings, crowned by a ridge roof. The roof is so slanted that the top floor is reduced to a loft which, in order to gain space, must project outwardly. This section and the bay window on the corner are the only curves, albeit very gentle and serene. The stuccoed whiteness of the walls invades the few garlands with different coloured sgraffiti. The railings, decorated with floral motifs, are painted in pale tonalities.

The house took part in the competition for the Town Hall prize yet only received a mention, for the award was bestowed upon another of his works, the Casarramona factory.

In 1940 it became the gynaecological clinic run by doctor Melcior Collet, though the conversion only required a new interior decoration, carried out by

Santiago Marco. In 1982 the doctor ceded it to the Generalitat on the condition that it were to house a museum of sport, which opened in 1986. This change propitiated a restoration, under the responsibility of Joan Bassegoda i Nonell who in addition to recuperating the original values, such as the white of the walls — though not the straw colour Cirici mentions — and the pale green of the railings, contributed another most appreciated novelty: the reappearance of sgraffiti in the form of the group of polychrome figures that had decorated the gable-end of the façade giving on to carrer Buenos Aires. The fact is that at the outbreak of the Civil War the Company family, fearing the retaliations of the Anarchists, gave instructions for this evocation of the Assumption of the Virgin Mary to be removed before it was violently destroyed. The present ochre colour of the walls is the result of a subsequent restoration.

Casimir Casarramona Factory

1911

Mèxic, 36, Barcelona

In 1907 the growing cotton industry founded by Casimir Casarramona, initially specialised in blankets and towels and then extended to include men's tailoring and First Communion outfits, thereby increasing its popularity, propitiated the purchase of a large plot of land on the slope of Montjuïc, at that time a remote and inhospitable area. In 1909 Puig i Cadafalch received the commission to undertake the project of building a factory, but in 1911 a fire completely destroyed the industry that had been originally established in carrer Riereta, a disastrous episode that obliged the architect to enlarge the sizeable construction being carried out.

This immense series of warehouses led Cirici to evoke his impression of Westminster, given the prominence of horizontal volumes with no other counterpoint than two elements of a pronounced verticality — the clock tower and the water-tower, both prolonged by fine spires. The former was used to hold advertising posters designed in a style and calligraphy similar to those of the architect Gallissà, who Puig i Cadafalch greatly respected. All the warehouses, extremely luminous and spacious, form a swell with the same rhythm and materials such as brick, stucco, artificial stone and ceramic. Such a spectacular display of thrilling exploitation of flat bricks to create the vaults, a technique imported from Italy in the 14th century and continually improved by Catalan masters, received unanimous praise.

This work was awarded the Town Hall prize to the best building of 1911.

Over the course of time it became the barracks of the armed police, though it was finally destined to house the headquarters of La Caixa Foundation and its exhibition centre, and consequently underwent a restoration that has dignified it.

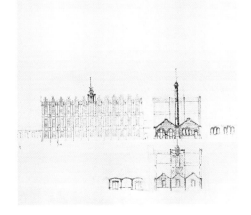

Elevation of the main façade (first version), 1903–1904

Interior, circa 1920

17

Casa Josep Puig i Cadafalch

1917

Provença, 231, Barcelona

The architect lived on the third floor of Gran Via de les Corts Catalanes, 604 (near carrer Balmes), until in 1917 he carried out the transformation and extension of a two-storey house belonging to the writer Dolors Monserdà, widow of Macià, his mother-in-law, constructed by the architect J. Pi i Calleja, a dwelling in which she only spent the summer as her usual residence was the house she owned in carrer Nou de Sant Francesc. The change entailed converting the house into a residence and studio, which the architect would occupy until his death at the age of 89 on the 23rd of December of 1956. Above a ground floor intended to house shops, the first floor was to be the mother-in-law's home, while the second floor would be his abode and studio. This place of work receives the light entering through a convex bay window that presents the subtle gentleness of Mackintosh, to avoid too much of a contrast with the purity and simplicity of the rest of the façade giving on to carrer Provença. Not having been erected between party walls, the house benefited from another side that vibrantly illuminates those rooms. The construction presents the typical roof of the environs, edged by a balustrade and enhanced by a pergola.

The front door is distinguished by the date printed in Roman numerals and by the sgraffiti of two figures holding the same number of objects revealing the spirit of our personage, a lyre and a compass evoking art and technique in an allusion to the architect and the graduate in Physics and Mathematics.

In short, this project betrays a certain influence of Mackintosh and the *Sezession*, although the architect Romeu stated it had closer affinity with Josep Maria Loos and Casa Steiner.

18

Casa Joan Pich i Pon

1921

Plaça de Catalunya, 9, Barcelona

Puig i Cadafalch was as familiar with this heart of the city as if it were his own home, for not in vain had he studied it paying great attention to detail after receiving the municipal commission to design a total renovation of such a symbolic square. So it must certainly have pleased him to be able to work on such an important project as that proposed by Joan Pich i Pon. This collaboration must no doubt have proved surprising and was widely discussed, for the industrial tycoon was a very popular man who inspired all sorts of stories that discredited him, presenting him unfairly as a fool. Yet we should realise that in spite of the architect's complex temperament the two men were neither enemies nor adversaries, merely political opponents. All the same, there is a key factor that enables us to understand this relationship between the member of the Lliga and the follower of Lerroux: they had met when they were both ministers and when Puig i Cadafalch became a member of the provincial government Pich i Pon, following the advice of Cambó, asked him to design the Exposition of Electrical Industries he was organising in Montjuïc. On the grand project of the Plaça de Catalunya they got on extremely well, as proven by the fact that after its completion he should have designed another for him, a huge building of houses on the attractive corner of Plaça Lesseps and avinguda República Argentina, where the industrialist's mistress would live.

This project consisted of the renovation and extension of the Narcís Pla house by the architect Francisco del Villar (the initiator of the Sagrada Familia) in 1875, that Pich i Pon had bought from the Batlló family that owned it at the time for two million pesetas. He added three more floors, culminating in the attic and penthouse in order to form a line with the neighbouring bulk of the Hotel Colón, which had also undergone an extension. The building is well oriented (it faces south), it is noteworthy (for its volume and situation) and attractive (as a result of the unusual grandeur of a space that favours an almost epic contemplation). It was the first group of offices erected in the Eixample, for until then they had been located on the Via Laietana. It was also the first time the owner did not occupy the mezzanine but the uppermost floor, as in America, and the first house to import this feature from the United States. Cirici investigated the influences and declared that the model inspiring Puig was that of Sullivan in Chicago — that of the Stock Exchange (1896), with its gentle play of curvatures and arcades on the lower part, that of the Carson department store (1899), with its large horizontal windows and that of the Auditorium (1896), because of the rhythm of its openings.

To facilitate the establishment of the offices the architect used a uniform paving, leaving each storey clear to enable neighbours to adapt them to their own needs. The front door is remarkable for its newly introduced Baroque style that will appear in subsequent works, possibly of either Valencian or French influence, a style repeated in the vases festooning the railings of the house. The lower parts of the templets crowning the building recall Valencian models, while the upper parts are reminiscent of the pink Ionic columns of the Labyrtinth of Horta. In spite of the numerous possible meanings, the life-size Hermes figures at the very top have been associated with the God of trade, though I myself am more inclined to see them as swift messengers, for Pich i Pon was the founder of two newspapers, *El día Gráfico* and *La Noche*, the editorial offices of which were housed in the building.

This splendid illustrated recreation of the School of Chicago which at the time symbolised the avant-garde, suffered inconsiderate mutilations, starting with the assault launched by the architect Bona when he erected his mediocre bank colossus after the Civil War, eliminating one of the templets in the process. The renovation of the building, carried out in two stages under the direction of the architect Jordi Romeu, has restored the dignity it had been deprived of in such a humiliating manner.

Plaça de Catalunya, circa 1933

19

Casa Lluís Guarro

1923

Via Laietana, 37, Barcelona

This building combines offices and dwellings and was commissioned by the historic and prestigious paper manufacturer, the origins of whose business dated back to the eighteenth century. The architect was well familiar with the site, having taken part as a town planner in the task of reconstructing part of the urban fabric that had given rise to the space, and above all to the Gothic legacy. The flavour of this project also reminds us of the modernity constructed in the city of skyscrapers. The high compact section rises above a ground plan structured by means of a base of columns and an entresol with five arches. The front door, made of stone and framed by columns, culminates with the generosity and profusion of the Baroque, expressed by the fruit and garlands brimming over the vase. The mezzanine is enhanced by a portico of columns, a continuous balustrade running along the length of the floor and crowned by six vases. The whole section of the building is governed by large horizontal windows that were one of the signs of the new modernity. The wrought-iron balconies were decorated with volutes inspired in the style of the eighteenth century. On the roof, as in the Virreina Palace, we find the same rhythm mentioned previously, created by a further six vases. The rear façade is simpler, made in the same style and of the same quality yet of a more radical nature and a rare intensity, crowned by a striking pergola supported by clustered columns.

20

Casa August Casarramona

1923

Passeig de Gràcia, 48, Barcelona

The youngest son of the founder of the textile industry previously mentioned commissioned this building, which he designed after having worked on the factory in Montjuïc and the renovation of an old house in carrer Sant Pere més Alt for the family. This project fits in with the style of Casa Guarro, although the latter reveals a more refined use of ornamentation and of the materials employed, transmitting a more sumptuous image as corresponds to the most important public space of the period and to its most exquisite area facing the Mançana de la Discòrdia that the architect knew well. He was also familiar with this area, as in 1902 he had designed the luxurious Hotel Términus nearby (no longer standing), the façade of which gave on to carrer Aragó directly in front of the railway station.

Sketch of an ornamental detail

The project consisted of the remodelling of a house belonging to a master builder constructed in the last decades of the previous century. The ground floor was devoted to the textile enterprise. The front door, in the middle, is framed by sturdy marble columns and brass capitals, while the lintel includes an impressive dangling garland made of bronze, representing fruit in the Baroque style of Trianon. The mezzanine is emphasised by a double line of continuous gallery with an sumptuous wrought-iron railing, and above all by a decorated bay window delicately carved in oak in an original manner. The top floor stands out as a result of its continuous balustrade, repeated above to festoon the roof, presenting the habitual resort of huge Baroque vases. This space was made into a roof garden. The exterior opulence was further highlighted by the decoration of the proprietor's flat, for whom Puig i Cadafalch designed furniture inspired by that of Louis XV in the Hall of Mirrors in Versailles.

It is worthwhile noting that the house would later be occupied by relatives of Vilató, the husband of Lola Picasso, sister of the painter. The fact that they should have kept everything the artist had left in his parent's home enabled this set of works, together with the Sabartés collection, to become the starting point of the Museu Picasso in carrer Montcada.

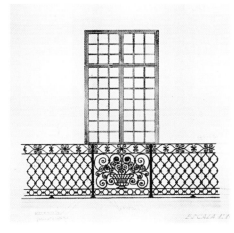

Detail of the balcony

21

Palau Alfons XIII and Palau Victòria Eugènia

1923

Plaça del Marquès de Foronda, Fira de Montjuïc, Barcelona

Promoted by Joan Pich i Pon and Cambó, Montjuïc was selected as the site for the celebration of the Exposition of Electrical Industries in 1917. Puig i Cadafalch was the architect chosen to design the development of such a large space, as well as some of the pavilions. His organising vision led him to be original and to leave a very personal stamp on the project, by dispensing with both the Gran Via and the Paral·lel avenues, as well as Via K conceived in the first design by Amargós, with the intention of concentrating the essential focal points in the following areas: Plaça Espanya as a prelude; avinguda Maria Cristina and avinguda Rius i Taulet as the main and secondary arteries of the central site; Miramar as a link to the harbour and the sea. In short, a scheme befitting Baroque town-planning, a design based on clear strong arteries that at the same time were also indebted to the style of Otto Wagner, despite the fact that previous world fairs such as the Parisian Exposition Universelle of 1900, had emphasised at least one basic artery of an epic grandeur. One of the important elements from the architectonic point of view was the peculiar evocation of the Vatican colonnade by Bernini, also expressed by an exhedra functioning as an arcade and by the palaces that would stand at the two sides of the avenue. The architect Romeu specifies that references can be found to Madison Square Garden, to the University of Columbia and the Museum of Fine Arts in Boston, as well as to the Generalife and to Valencian scenography, all recreated naturally according to our architect's talent and personality.

The crossroads of the two avenues (Maria Cristina and Rius i Taulet), at the origin of the first large elevated plane (where the Magic Fountain was subsequently located by those who replaced Puig i Cadafalch on the project) was the symbolic and representational spot where he ordered the placing of four giant columns, measuring twenty metres high, to be crowned by the same number of winged victories symbolising the four stripes of the Catalan flag and which, according to Romeu, he had seen at the West Point Academy on one of his many trips to the United States lecturing at different universities. The four columns were subsequently demolished — not blown up by the burning of wooden wedges previously introduced in them — following military orders, for the fact is that the Exposition should have been inaugurated in 1917 yet suffered repeated

Study for the door of the main entrance to the Palace of Fine Arts, 1920

postponements until the *coup d'état* of 1923, when General Primo de Rivera proclaimed his dictatorship. Puig i Cadafalch handed in his resignation as President of the Mancomunitat de Catalunya, a situation which led to his being replaced as director of the project, that would finally become the future World Fair of 1929.

The only elements that had remained standing and intact — his town planning project was respected albeit with a few changes of varying sign and scope — were the two palaces of Alfons XIII and Victòria Eugènia that had already been constructed under his personal direction. They are without a shadow of doubt the best buildings of the whole development. To begin with, they occupy the best position as regards the topography of the area, and their symmetry benefits the two constructions and their surroundings. Then again, their interior space is the most appropriate for each need, as they are susceptible of adapting to the demands of each particular event, to highly advantageous results. Moreover, the quality of the natural lighting is excellent. While the Alfons XIII palace was erected by means of a metallic structure, which endowed it with a light-weight, transparent interior nurtured by a diffused and well-distributed zenithal light, the Victòria Eugènia palace was built with a socle made up of pieces of a novel concrete pre-fabricated on the site itself, which resulted in the rich play of arcs and columns. After having rehearsed several proposals for the façades he decided upon solid walls stuccoed in gold, and instead of placing a rhythm of more or less free-standing columns, he preferred the originality of expressing them by means of the two-tone sgraffito that enhances a sensual spirally twisted shaft (Salomónica) peopled with flowers, while the angles of the building were crowned by delicate templets reminiscent of Valencian models.

22

Casa Muley-Afid

1911

Passeig de la Bonanova, 55, Barcelona

The origin of this villa is closely related to a delightful exotic character, the one-time sultan of Morocco. Dethroned by his brother, he sought refuge in our city, which welcomed him affectionately. Wishing to show his indebtedness he purchased a new elephant for the zoo, bereft of such a species since the death of its beloved Avi. The Town Hall organised a children's parade as a token of gratitude for his gesture, and a photograph secured the indescribable image of the youngsters standing under the balcony from where he was cheered while he threw sweets and coins down to them. All this took place in Hotel Oriente, in the middle of the Rambla, as he still did not have a house of his own. Enchanted by Barcelona and madly in love with the popular singer Carmen Flores, he longed for the intimacy only a private residence could afford and thus entrusted Puig i Cadafalch with the project to build one for him. At that time the Bonanova avenue was secluded enough to meet his needs, and the outcome was a villa in keeping with those that had been festooning such an opulent area since the turn of the century.

A wall of unhewn stone and a simple railing protect the garden surrounding this town house. It consists of a set of different volumes articulated with some complexity, which perhaps detracts from its slenderness despite the architect's endeavours to counteract such an effect by means of the willowy tower crowned by a long spire. Although the walls were stuccoed in white and the ochre-coloured sgraffiti are austere, the brick and the ceramic tiles offset the image of clarity and joie de vivre characterising similar dwellings.

Fortunately, the fact that the villa had been catalogued avoided it being demolished at a time when an excessive taste for speculation prevailed along this powerful artery, though it did doom the building to a state of neglect. At the onset of the new century a process of renovation was undertaken which has thus far spoilt part of the garden.

Biography

Ramon Casas. *Portrait of Josep Puig i Cadafalch*, ca. 1906.

1867
Josep Puig i Cadafalch is born on the 17th of October in Mataró, within a wealthy family of textile industrialists.

1883
He studies Architecture and Exact Sciences at the University of Barcelona and at the age of 21 is awarded a doctorate by the University of Madrid.

1886
He joins the newly-founded Centre Escolar Catalanista, which he will preside over from 1888 to 1890.

1891
He becomes a qualified architect at the age of 24.

1892
Puig i Cadafalch is named municipal architect of Mataró (1892–1896), where he designs the town hall project for the city's sewer system.

1893
In Barcelona he begins the construction of one of his most popular works, Casa Terradas or the House of Thorns.

1895
The architect establishes himself in Barcelona and secures one of his first important commissions, Casa Francesc Martí i Puig, which would subsequently house the café-beer tavern Els Quatre Gats. This marks the beginning of a vast number of works and projects, which he combines with activity in the fields of politics, archaeology, teaching and art history.

1901–1903
Puig i Cadafalch is elected councillor of the Barcelona Town Hall, and from 1901 to 1902 occupies a position as lecturer at the School of Architecture of Barcelona.

1908
He launches the project of archaeological excavations in Empúries, and during the years to come will take part personally in over fifteen excavations in different sites.

1907–1909
During these years he is elected a member of parliament for Barcelona in Madrid.

1909–1918
Puig publishes *L'arquitectura romànica a Catalunya*, with A. de Folguera and J. Goday.

1913–1924
Elected as a member of the provincial government for Barcelona.

1917–1924
Following another election he becomes President of the Mancomunitat de Catalunya.

1923
He is awarded Honorary Degrees by the universities of Friburg (1923), Paris (1930) and Toulouse (1949).

1925–1930
Puig lectures at the Sorbonne (1925), at Harvard and Cornell (1926), and at the Institut d'Art et Archéologie in Paris (1930).

1930
The architect publishes *La geografia i els orígens del primer romànic*.

1932
He publishes *La place de la Catalogne dans la geographie et la chronologie du premier art roman*.

1935
L'architecture gothique civil en Catalogne is his next publication.

1936
He goes into exile in France, where he remains until 1942.

1949
He publishes *L'escultura romànica a Catalunya*.

1957
Puig i Cadafalch dies in Barcelona on the 23rd of December.

Chronology of works and projects by Puig i Cadafalch

The initials OB and JBN refer to the dating carried out by Oriol Bohigas and Joan Bassegoda i Nonell in their works, cited in the bibliography of this volume.

1892
Mataró to Ripoll commemorative flag.
Tablet commissioned by Unió Catalanista to commemorate the work of bishop Morgades on the reconstruction of Ripoll.
Ornamental urns for the remains of Counts Guifré el Pelós and Ramon Berenguer III, Ripoll.
Casa Sisternes, Mataró (OB).
Palomer shop, Mataró (OB).
Plaça Major market-place, Mataró (OB).
Provisional market-place, Mataró.
Restoration of the stone cross marking the municipal boundary, Mataró (JBN).
Casa Valls, Mataró (JBN).

1892–1896
Outdoor festival decorations, Mataró.

1893
Sisternes Urbanisation, Mataró.
Can Titus Spa, Caldes d'Estrac.

1893–1894
Macià Jewellers, Barcelona. No longer standing.

1894
Renovation of La Benificència rest-home (at present Red Cross), Mataró (OB).
Casa Parera, Mataró (OB).
Refuge for shipwrecked victims, Mataró, ca. 1894.

1895
Flag in homage to Pons i Gallarza on occasion of the Jocs Florals [Poetry Festival] (OB).
Sewer system, Mataró.
Casa Alfred Riera, Barcelona.

1895–1896
Casa Pere i Francesc Martí i Puig (Els 4 Gats), Barcelona.

1896
La Confiança shop, Mataró.
Joan Macià family vault, Barcelona (JBN).
V Misteri de dolor [Mystery of Sorrow] monumental bead and red, Montserrat monastery (OB).
Anís del Mono kiosk, Badalona railway station.

1897
Damm i Montells family vault, Barcelona (OB, JBN).
Project for a monument to Rius i Taulet.
Casa Moreu, Agell (JBN).
Mercantile Club, Mataró.

1897–1905
Casa Josep Puig i Cadafalch, Argentona.

1897–1898
Casa Joaquim Coll i Regàs, Mataró.

1898
Casa Josep Garí (El Cros), Argentona (OB, JBN 1899–1900).
Hospice and cross, Misericòrdia hermitage, Canet de Mar (OB, JBN, 1902).
Chapel and cross, Verge de Gràcia hermitage, Lloret de Mar (OB).
Casas family vault, Sant Feliu de Guíxols (OB).
Altar reredos, Santíssim Sagrament chapel, Vilassar de Dalt (JBN).

1898–1900
Casa Antoni Amatller, Barcelona.
Casa Romà Macaya, Barcelona (JBN, OB 1901).
La Veu de Catalunya offices, Barcelona.
Casa Eusebi Bofill, Viladrau (OB 1900; JBN 1904).
III Misteri de goig [Mystery of Joy] monumental bead and red, Montserrat monastery.

1900
Casa Antoni Fernández (Napoleó), Barcelona (JBN).
Stand for the Comas Blanch knitwear factory (Mataró) at the Paris Exposition.

1900–1903
Baró de Quadras castle, Massanes.

1901
Tibidabo Restaurant. Project.
Ferran Laboratory. Project.

1901–1902
Casa Lluís Muntades, Barcelona.
Casa Martí i Puig, Barcelona.

1901–1904
Codorniu Cellars, Sant Sadurní d'Anoia (JBN, OB 1904).

1901–1907
Casa Pere Serra i Pons, Barcelona.

1902
Interior designs at Labat, Biarritz.
Furriol cottage, La Garriga (JBN, OB 1902–1903).
Capella villa, Sant Gervasi de Cassoles, Barcelona.
Torino bar, Barcelona (JBN). No longer standing.
Hotel Términus, Barcelona (JBN, OB 1902–1903). No longer standing.
Palau Baró de Quadras, Barcelona (JBN, OB 1904).
Costa i Macià family vault, Lloret de Mar.

1902–1904
Casa Avel·lí Trinxet, Barcelona. No longer standing.

1903
Casa Riera i Puig, Viladrau (JBN).
Casa Mercè Pastor de Cruylles, Barcelona.
Terradas farmhouse (Sobrevia), Seva.
Caballol villa, Barcelona (JBN).
Stone landmark and cross marking the municipal boundary, Sant Pere del Bosc, Lloret de Mar (JBN).

1903–1904
Casa Concepció Dolsa (widow of Llorach), Barcelona. No longer standing.
First Casimir Casarramona factory, Barcelona, ca. 1903–1904.
First Carbonell i Susana factory, Canet de Mar, ca. 1903–1904.

1903–1905
Casa Bartomeu Terradas i Brutau (Casa de les Punxes), Barcelona.
Terradas family vault, Barcelona (OB).
Garí family vault, Esplugues de Llobregat (OB).

1904
Casa Polo, Barcelona (OB).
Baró de Quadras family vault, Barcelona (OB).
Cog railway station, Montserrat.

1905
Casa Maresch de Casarramona, Tàrrega.
Casa Doctor Francesc Sastre i Marquès, Barcelona (OB).
Can Feliu, Vilassar.

1905–1906
Sastre i Marquès Pharmacy, Barcelona.

1906
Casa Raventós (Can Codorniu Villa), Sant Sadurní d'Anoia.
Casa F. Mercader, Barcelona (JBN).

Palais de la Paix, The Hague, Holland.
Restoration of the apse, Sant Martí Sarroca (JBN).
Casa Macià/Macaya, Barcelona. Project.

1908
Queen's throne and hall decoration for the Jocs
Florals [Poetry festival].
Iron and ceramic fountain, Palace of Fine Arts,
Barcelona.

1908–1909
Votive church, Buenos Aires. Project.

1909
Casa Ángeles Macià i Monserdà, Sarrià, Barcelona.
Marconi Telegraph Office. Location unknown,
ca. 1909.

1909–1911
Casimir Casarramona Factory, Barcelona.

1910
Interior design of the hall devoted to the
Promotion of National Labour, Spanish Pavilion,
Exposition Universelle, Brussels.
Monument to Víctor Balaguer (JBN).
Casa Bofarull, near Madrid.
Julio Vicente Tejidos shop, Valladolid, ca. 1910.

1911
Casa Pere Company, Barcelona.
Lampposts, Barcelona (JBN).
Casa Muley-Afid, Barcelona (OB), ca. 1911.

1911–1912
Casa Joan Serratosa Albert, Barcelona.

1911–1914
Competition for a new post-office. Project.
Layout of the area surrounding the Cathedral
and Plaça del Rei in the Gothic quarter,
Barcelona. Project.

1912
Ballarín i Cia workshop and office, Barcelona.
Monument to Milà i Fontanals, Vilafranca del
Penedès (JBN).

1912–1917
Restoration of Sant Joan de les Abadesses.

1913
Miele Jewellers, Barcelona. No longer standing.
Casa Joaquim Carreras, Sarrià, Barcelona. No
longer standing.

Renovation of a house in carrer Montcada,
Barcelona.

1914
Interior renovation of the Palau de la Generalitat
to house the Biblioteca de Catalunya (OB).
Design of bronze lanterns for the courtyard of
the Llotja de Mar, Barcelona (JBN).
Renovation of Sr. Garí's flat, Barcelona (JBN).
Swimming-pool for Mr. Pearson, USA (JBN).
Project.
Garden City, Monte del Pardo. Project.

1915
Interior design of Esteve Andorrà Locksmiths,
Barcelona (JBN, OB: 1916?).

1915–1923
Urban layout of the Plaça de Catalunya,
Barcelona. Project.

1917
Macià family vault, Barcelona (OB).
Casa Josep Puig i Cadafalch, Barcelona.
"Colla de l'arròs" house, Montjuïc, Barcelona.
Casa Sra. Jover i Llisach (widow of Guix),
Santpedor.
Renovation of the monastery library, Montserrat.
Monument to Prat de la Riba, ca. 1917. Project.
Casa Pilar Moragas, Viladecans, ca. 1917.

1917–1924
Exposition of Electrical Industries, Montjuïc,
Barcelona. Project.

1918
Casa Fargas (El Maset), either in Sant Quirze de
Safaja or in Sant Feliu de Codines.
Reform of Barcelona: Plans with additions made
by Puig in pencil, a plan for a municipal theatre
and a new street.
Old Casarramona flat, Barcelona.

1919
Casa Joaquim Carreras, Barcelona, ca. 1919.

1919–1920
Casa Joan Pich i Pon, Barcelona.

1920
Restoration of the Sant Pere church, Terrassa.
Ybern workers' residential development. Project.
Filipines restaurant, kiosk, Barcelona, ca. 1920.
Project.

1920–1921
Workers' Bazaar, Sants, Barcelona.
Extension (2 storeys) of Casa Estanislau Segarra, Barcelona.

1920–1925
Urban development of Sant Andreu de Llavaneres. Project.

1921
Small house by the station, Llavaneres.

1922–1923
Casa Casimir Casarramona, Barcelona.
Casa Lluís Guarro, Barcelona.

1923
Casa Guarro, Barcelona.
Casa Pich, Sant Vicenç de Llavaneres.
Brutau family vault, Barcelona.
Casa Garí, Barcelona, ca. 1923.

1923–1924
Renovation of Casa Maria Guarro, Barcelona.

1923–1928
New cloister, façade, garage, refectory, approach road and monument to Abbot Oliba, Montserrat monastery.

1924
Francesc Cambó family vault, Barcelona.

1924–1928
Baldachin and pedestal for the Mare de Déu del Claustre, Solsona.

1925
Freixas altar. Location unknown.
Montserdà altar, Sabadell, ca. 1925.

1926
Small building in Cambridge, Massachusetts, USA, ca. 1926.

1927
Shop in Passeig de Gràcia, Barcelona.

1927–1930
Restoration and consolidation of Santa Cecília de Montserrat.

1928–1929
Casa Rosa Alemany, Barcelona.

1928–1932
Casa Pich i Pon, Barcelona.

1929
Shelter in carrer de l'Àguila for Josep Maria Carbó, Barcelona (JBN).
Casino, Argentona.

1930
Montserdà family vault.
Monument to Mistral, Montjuïc, Barcelona.

1930–1931
Installation of the Institut d'Estudis Catalans in Santa Creu Hospital, Barcelona.

1931
Monument to Àngel Guimerà, Barcelona. Project.

1932
Interior renovation of the house belonging to the widow of Enric Prat de la Riba, Barcelona.

1933–1935
Santa Creu Hospital, Barcelona. Redesigning of the gardens.

1934
Valldaura family vault.

1936
Conversion of the new sacristy of the Poblet monastery into a Pantheon of Illustrious Catalans. Project.

1939
Altar of the Santíssima, Argentona, ca. 1939.

1940–1942
Hotel for Sr. La Cruz, Les Escaldes, Andorra.

1942
Dels Dolors chapel and Sant Pere altar, Santa Maria church, Mataró.

1944
Renovation of Casa Guarro, Alella (JBN).

1945
Chapel and other quarters in the Sta Teresa convent school, housed in what was formerly Casa Pere Serra i Pons, Rambla de Catalunya 126, Barcelona (JBN).

1947
Altar, Capuchin convent, Mataró (JBN).

Bibliography

Various authors, *Centenari d'Els Quatre Gats*, Barcelona, 1997.

Bassegoda i Nonell, Joan, *Puig i Cadafalch*, Barcelona: Gent Nostra Series, no. 42, Edicions de Nou Art Thor, 1998².

Alcolea i Gil, Santiago, *Petita història de Puig i Cadafalch*, Barcelona: Editorial Mediterrània, 2001².

Bohigas, Oriol, *Arquitectura modernista*. Photographs by Leopoldo Pomés, Barcelona: Editorial Lumen, 1968.

— *Reseña y Catálogo de la Arquitectura Modernista*, Vols. I, II, Barcelona: La palabra del tiempo Series, nos. 149 & 150, Editorial Lumen, 1983.

Cabré, Tate, *Guia de la Ruta del modernisme: Barcelona oest, Canet de Mar*, Barcelona: Editorial Mediterrània, 2000.

Cirici Pellicer, Alexandre, *El arte modernista catalán*, Barcelona: Editorial Aymà, 1951.

Freixa, Mireia; Mercader, Laura and Molet, Joan, *Catàleg de la Ruta Europea del Modernisme*, Barcelona: Editorial Mediterrània, 2000.

González, Antoni and Lacuesta, Raquel, *Guía de Arquitectura Modernista Europea*, Barcelona: Editorial Gustau Gili, 1997³.

Jardí i Casany, Enric, *Puig i Cadafalch. Arquitecte, polític i historiador de l'art*, Mataró: Caixa d'Estalvis Laietana, 1975.

— *A Stroll Through Modernista Barcelona*. Photographs by Melba Levick, Barcelona: Edicions Polígrafa, 1998.

Pi de Cabanyes, Oriol, *Cases modernistes de Catalunya*, Barcelona: Edicions 62, 1992.

Rohrer, Judith; De Solà-Morales, Ignasi; Barral, Xavier and Termes, Josep, *Catàleg de l'exposició J. Puig i Cadafalch: L'arquitectura entre la casa i la ciutat*, Barcelona: Fundació Caixa de Pensions and Col·legi d'Arquitectes de Catalunya, 1989.

Vila-Grau, Joan and Rodon, Francesc, *Els vitrallers de la Barcelona modernista*, Barcelona: Edicions Polígrafa, 1982.